CW01673886

UNSTOPPABLE WOMEN

Female Entrepreneurs'
Stories To Inspire And Motivate

To Ems
Continue to be the
Unstoppable, Kind &
Inspiring Women

GRISELDA TOGOBO

You are!

Love Chrissy x

Copyright © 2022 Griselda Togobo

The rights of Griselda Togobo to be identified as the author of this work have been asserted in accordance with the Copyright, Designs and Patents Act 1988. All rights reserved.

Except for the quotation of small passages for the purposes of criticism and review, no part of this publication may be reproduced, stored in a retrieval system, or transmitted, in any form or by any means, electronic, mechanical, photocopying, recording or otherwise, except under the terms of the Copyright, Designs and Patents Act 1988, and without the prior consent of the author.

A record of this book is available from the British Library.

Soar Publishing

ISBN: 978-1-9196168-0-3

Praise for Unstoppable Women

"Inspiring! If you are seeking a read to motivate your entrepreneurial journey, driven by incredible true stories of innovative female founders, this is the book for you! Authentic in style, sharing great value."

– Scarlett Allen-Horton, Director,
Harper Fox Partners, BBC Apprentice Finalist,
Business Partner to Lord Sugar.

"This book is full of practical advice for any woman looking to realise their entrepreneurial dreams."

– Kavita Oberoi OBE, Secret Millionaire.

"An inspiring book full of business tips and strategies. This is a must-read for every woman starting, scaling or thinking of exiting their business. It's a valuable opportunity to discover the shortcuts from other women entrepreneurs, so you arrive at your destination faster."

– Stephanie J. Hale BEM,
author of *Millionaire Women, Millionaire You.*

"This book has inspired me tremendously and opened my eyes to myriad possibilities I would never have considered – before I read it, I thought I'd missed my chance to try launching a business from scratch, but this book has proven beyond a doubt that you can never say never, and that the only thing that is holding you back is you. I recommend it highly to anyone who has ever had the inklings of a business idea, or dared to dream – this book will be an invaluable roadmap."

– Jane Cahane, Journalist.

Thank you to the unstoppable women at www.forwardladies.com for providing the inspiration for this book.

This book is dedicated to my mother, Comfort – a consummate entrepreneur – for her excellent example and modelling of what it means to be unstoppable, and to all the amazing unstoppable women featured here.

Thank you to my wonderful husband Michael and our children, Makavo and Elinam, for supporting me through it all.

TABLE OF CONTENTS

ABOUT THE AUTHOR

Griselda Togobo MPhil, ACA, is an international corporate consultant and trainer. She is also a multi-faceted entrepreneur, engineer and chartered accountant. At her core, she is a commercially focused business consultant, but her experience as a black woman in the corporate world drives her. She now uses her vast international experience to help progressive global companies create inclusive workplaces. Griselda gives keynotes, talks and workshops to businesses interested in improving the gender and racial diversity of their teams.

Her corporate programmes include leadership development, equity, diversity and inclusion training and private coaching for senior management. She works directly with CEOs, business leaders and managers to close the gender and ethnicity gaps in their organisations.

She is a respected and impactful speaker and is known for her high energy and engaging style.

As an expert in diversity and inclusion, Science, Technology, Engineering & Maths (STEM), leadership development and entrepreneurship, Griselda offers a fresh approach to diversity in leadership development.

She qualified as a chartered accountant with Deloitte LLP and has an MPhil in Industrial Systems, Manufacture and Management from Wolfson College, Cambridge University. Griselda is a Teaching Fellow at Lancaster University, a doctoral researcher at Strathclyde University, sits on the Law & Business School Advisory Board at Leeds Beckett University and the Yorkshire Leadership Group of the Prince's Trust, Mosaic Network.

Griselda is passionate about supporting female leaders through www.forwardladies.com, a 20,000-strong (and growing) professional women's network.

She lives in Yorkshire with her husband and two children.

Griseldatogobo.com
Instagram: griseldatogobo
LinkedIn: griseldatogobo
Facebook: griseldatogoboFL
Twitter: griseldatogobo

ALSO BY GRISELDA TOGOBO

How To Become An Expert In 7 Simple Steps: Build A Business Around What You Already Know And Get Highly Paid For It.

Rip Up Your To-Do List: Discover Time Management Principles That Will Transform Your Life And Business.

The Goal Achiever Planner – www.goalachieverplanner.com.

FOREWORD BY
DAME STEPHANIE SHIRLEY CH

I love these stories for their focus on success and because they feature women (too often portrayed as the weaker sex). These are strong women who understand the obstacles that lie before them. And know they are surmountable.

Women in the world economy are all sorts of people and have little in common. Except perhaps that we are all drawn to the challenges of the 21st century. It's a good century for women, the power shift to social networks plays to our traditional strengths.

There are women entrepreneurs in stereotypical female areas such as fashion and skincare but there are far more of us in finance, in media and in technology that is absorbing all of business.

The heart of any business is about making things happen. That's only worthwhile if done with sensitivity to social issues. It is people, not organisations, who make the world go round. It is people – with all our strengths and failings – who are the powerhouse at every level of life. The creative spark for new enterprise comes from people. It's their drive that brings an enterprise to life. Their professionalism and dedication to quality that makes an enterprise flourish.

It's one thing to have an idea for an enterprise. As most readers know, to then make it happen requires extraordinary energy, self-belief and perseverance; the courage to risk family and home; and a 24/7 commitment that borders on the obsessive.

The relentless drive for efficiency; the ongoing attack on costs; the pursuit of excellence – they are all an essential part of the business process. It's a learning experience. Money borrowed to scary levels. How and when to take risks. How to select, train and manage staff. And how to turn them into partners. How to lead. Women are no longer the exception but we are still far from "the rule" in terms of leadership. And you cannot be a leader unless you act. Thinking is not enough.

Of course, we enjoy things we're good at and are good at the things we enjoy. Apart from the time commitment, there's a vital need to go further, to see the broader picture. This means more than having a personal goal like "I wannabe rich". It means having goals for your community, your profession and your country.

To be able to go beyond oneself, you need a healthy selfishness. To invest in yourself – your mind, body and spirit – to ensure your own self-preservation and development. Success is often found at the very edge of failure.

Always, always, it is teamwork that carries forward the vision. In both my working life and since my nominal retirement, I delegate the execution of my vision to others. And gain personal strength by embracing the concept of empowerment. As with love, it is more about giving than taking. Each team needs to recognise its own power. As the Chinese philosopher Lao Tsu put it: "The leader did nothing, we did it all ourselves".

My advice on starting an entrepreneurial journey is to concentrate on something you know and care about; get enough experience and training to take you to the leading edge; then grasp the risk and commit to the project. (If it fails, you can always try something else!)

So, be the very best you can and in your own way. Let sexist prejudice roll off you. It can even be an advantage. Among the multitude of men, those of us present are more likely to be remembered.

Nowadays, the men fight with us.

DAME STEPHANIE is a workplace revolutionary turned venture philanthropist. A serial entrepreneur, in 1962 she set up a disruptive software business originally biased towards women that she took to co-ownership, making 70 of her staff into millionaires; and later four charities (taking three to sustainability and together employing over 1000 people).

Every penny Dame Stephanie receives from sales of her books, *Let It Go* and *So To Speak*, goes to *Autistica* – order via www.steveshirley.com.

INTRODUCTION

I have read many business books aimed at female entrepreneurs. They are typically inspirational, but sometimes unrelatable. Once entrepreneurs achieve a certain level of success, the trappings of wealth will inevitably make their daily lives appear so different from those of the rest of us that we can easily assume their lives are near perfect. But is this really the case?

The women we find most inspiring are inspirational not only because of their achievements and the heights they have reached in business, but also because of their humanity. The most inspiring women are those we can relate to, who we feel are just like us. They are women who have found the courage, strength and resilience to keep moving forward despite the challenges they face on this humbling journey we call life. They are the unstoppable ones.

No matter how successful they are, female entrepreneurs can still experience discrimination as women trying to move forward in what is still largely a man's world. They will still have sleepless nights over cash flow, staffing issues and the future of their businesses. For many of these women, the idea of a work-life balance remains elusive.

It is for these reasons I believe there is an audience for yet another book that shares not only the highs, but also the lows many women have faced during their entrepreneurial journey. As an entrepreneur myself, I am inspired by these women, which is why one of my life's greatest honours is running my women's network, www.forwardladies.com. I've met some wonderful women through this community of female leaders, and it brings me great pleasure to share their success stories with you.

Every woman featured in this book is a fantastic role model and successful by any definition of success, yet most of them still face their fair share of daily personal challenges, despite their success. None of them has achieved their success without having to slay a few personal dragons along the way.

This book is not a textbook on starting a business. There are already plenty of books on the market to help you with the details of how to do that. Instead, it's intended to inspire you and give you the confidence you need to become unstoppable in pursuing your own entrepreneurial goals.

The women featured in this book come from all walks of life – just like the women who live next door to you. The only difference about these women is that they didn't stop when others stopped. They kept going and persevered despite adversity, which is how they managed to achieve the successes they now enjoy. Some of these women may not yet be household names, but the majority featured in this book have achieved businesses that turn over millions of pounds each year, and have built up companies from the ground up.

When reading the stories, I was struck by how many of these women admitted to lacking confidence throughout their entrepreneurial journey. These are all highly successful women by any definition of the word, and yet some still find their confidence dips now and again, despite their success and the self-confidence they project to the outside world. Developing self-confidence and overcoming a sense of being an imposter are significant issues for women from all walks of life throughout their careers – however, as these stories of women who kept going and remained unstoppable reveal, confidence issues needn't hold any woman back from pursuing her dreams. You can still achieve success without being or feeling confident all the time. True unflappable confidence is a myth.

This book highlights the highs and lows of these women's journeys, including the valuable lessons each has learned along the way. Many of the women featured said they would gladly make all the same mistakes all over again because they appreciate what their experiences taught them. Their successes have not just been about the destination, but the journey.

For some of the women, I have focused on their start-up stories; for others, the focus is on the scale-up, and for a few the focus is on how they exited their business. Each chapter describes their journey into entrepreneurship, including the initial idea, key decisions and sacrifices made along the way. Some also share the systems and tools that have revolutionised their businesses, and how they manage their day-to-day lives to keep stress levels at bay. Each chapter ends with the featured woman's favourite saying, a low moment, a high moment, a golden nugget of take-away wisdom and a piece of advice to others who are just beginning their journey.

You can choose to read the book from cover to cover, or instead just pick out the sections that are the most relevant to you. As these stories show, it is tough running a business, but the most crucial thing to take away – although it is difficult, it is still possible – is that, ultimately, the rewards far exceed the risks and the sacrifices. Like my mother, a single mother of seven, entrepreneurship for many of these women is a matter of survival. Seeing my mother running her business instilled in me the can-do attitude and independence that would eventually lead me to venturing into entrepreneurship when I had my first child. I started my own business by registering a domain and website with £250, which has been the best investment I ever made in my life.

Our generation of women are living in the golden age of entrepreneurship with technology enabling businesses to innovate and reach new markets democratising access to opportunity and economic prosperity to all. We are living in an era where Bumble, the dating app for millennials, a company catering to women and led by women has just made its 31-year-old female founder Whitney Wolfe one of the youngest ever self-made billionaires.

I hope this book sparks ideas for your business journey. I hope it will give you the courage to take the next steps towards creating your own success story, and become as unstoppable as each of the women featured here. Be unstoppable.

Griselda Togobo

THE RELUCTANT ENTREPRENEUR

I'm not one of those who knew that I always wanted to be an entrepreneur. The one thing I knew with certainty growing was that I did not want to be an entrepreneur – both my parents run their businesses, and I saw first-hand hand how challenging it was to run companies and to build teams. I thought a more sensible approach would be getting a great degree to have my pick of corporate jobs and opportunities. I knew these corporate jobs paid well so, unlike my parents, I could earn a decent living and head home at the end of the day without carrying the stresses around like I saw my parents do.

So that is exactly what I did. I got the education and the job in corporate UK and started my journey climbing the corporate ladder.

My plan was that, once I reached the executive ranks, I would seamlessly introduce children into the mix and not miss a beat as I continued my ascent of the corporate ladder. I completely misjudged how I would feel once I became a mother. When my first child arrived, I realized that my whole life's dream needed to change to accommodate this little bundle of joy. I wanted my life to change to prioritise him. My ambition for my career did not wane but I now had this additional need be a parent that prioritised my son's well-being along my own career ambitions. I had a chat with the senior partner at the firm about working more flexibly, and he refused my request for flexible working. The incident was pivotal in my decision to exit the corporate world. I decided that I wouldn't be able to achieve my dreams at a firm that did not value my need for work and home life integration. I left to create my own company – somewhere that I could achieve this work and family life integration.

I also believe that seeing my parents running their own businesses made it possible for me to take this leap. Looking back, I had no idea what I had let myself in for. I read a few books on running a business and that was the extent of my education as an entrepreneur.

I had friends who laughed at my face when I shared my ideas with them, so I stopped sharing my ideas because I just could not take the ridicule. I was already filled with doubt at the idea of leaving a solid career to chase dreams that were notoriously difficult to achieve.

With my child, who was now six months old, I started my first company. And the rest, as they say, is history. My entrepreneurial journey has been anything but straightforward. I've had my fair share of challenges and setbacks – both personal and business-wise – and I've failed more times than I have succeeded. I keep failing every day as every day is a school-day when you are trying to grow a business.

I started my business journey with no contacts, no money or practical know-how. I had years of theoretical academic education and training, but nothing prepares you for life as an entrepreneur.

The beginning, the start-up phase, is the toughest. I was always stressed: juggling family life with the demands of a new start-up. I don't believe I excelled at either of these roles. In fact I was constantly feeling as though I was failing at both roles. The challenge of running a business impacted every area of my life including relationships, health, and wellbeing. I worked so hard and long during the early days that I spent the evenings treating myself to unhealthy comfort food.

As I grew my business and reputation, I realized that I needed to focus and invest more on myself and my personal development just as I was investing in the business. I needed to develop a mindset that would render me unstoppable. I also needed to become better at delegating and the need for scale required a whole different approach and mindset.

I was full of doubt and not always confident about what I was doing, although I am told that I always appeared super-confident. I guess I learnt to feel the fear and to do it anyway – as Susan Jeffers encourages us to do in her book *Feel The Fear And Do It Anyway.*

After all these years, constantly pushing myself out of my comfort zone is now the norm rather than the exception. The fear never goes away. However, I learnt to silence my inner critic and self-talk and to be kinder and more compassionate to myself.

When running a business, no two days are the same. My working day tends to start after I've dropped the children off at school at eight am. My business is run completely remotely. I made this transition to remote working after reading the book *REWORK* by Jason Fried and David Heinemeier Hansson. I now have systems in place to support my ambitions to remain a completely virtual team.

Today, my company is dedicated to helping organizations and individuals achieve their true potential by creating inclusive workplaces. I work with clients working in knowledge and technical industries such as engineering, technology, manufacturing, aerospace etc., which tend to be male-dominated.

The highs have been extraordinarily high, and the lows match their intensity too. My lowest point was waking up and realizing that I had not achieved the balance I sought when I left my well-paid corporate job to start my business—that awareness led to the decision to give up my office and to take my business completely virtual. That dark moment turned out to be the best decision giving me and my family a better integrated work and home life. Every day remains a school day.

SECTION 1: STARTING OUT

She believed she could – and so she did

We have all heard that one in ten start-ups don't make it past the first year, and only 10% of businesses survive after ten years. These statistics act as a cautionary tale to anyone thinking about starting their own business.

Only the brave – or those some will call the foolhardy – take the bold step into starting a business. These days, more women are starting businesses than ever before. The easy access to technology is a huge factor.

In this section of the book, I have focused on the start-up journeys of some incredible women. These are the ones who chose to dance to their own drumbeat and to chase their dreams of starting their own business. They chose to bring their ideas to life.

It always starts with an idea and the confidence to take the plunge. So, what did these women do differently with their ideas? Why did their ideas succeed when those of others failed?

Most successful entrepreneurs seem to stumble onto their business ideas due to their frustrations with current products or services in the market. So, you could start by asking yourself what you are frustrated about. What products and services would you like to see made?

Sara Blakely, the founder of Spanx and one of the world's first and youngest self-made billionaires, stumbled across her idea after she cut the legs of her tights off to create a revolutionary new product that we all now love – the Spanx. Our own Harriet Kelsall decided to bring her own ethically sourced, bespoke-designed jewellery to the masses after she spotted a gap in the market while working as a jewellery designer.

Both women kept putting one foot in front of the other and were committed to learning the skills they needed to develop their businesses and ideas along the way. This eventually led to the successes they now enjoy. Eventually, both of them learned innovative ways of marketing their businesses, building their personal brands, managing their cash flows and building their teams. They may not always have had the confidence to start a business, but their passion and enthusiasm for their products carried them through.

These women did not always start with millions in the bank; some started with only a few hundred pounds and others dipped into their savings. The key thing to remember when starting a business is that you have to have an alternative source of income, financial support from your family or a nest egg sufficient to give you the headspace to keep working on your idea until it gains traction.

Are you ready to begin your start-up journey?

1
YOU TOO CAN CREATE AN INNOVATIVE HAIRCARE PRODUCT

Be brave. You too can learn to fly and even soar like an eagle.

Rebecca McCann – Pro Blo Group

Not many entrepreneurs would say, "I owe my success to a broken hairbrush." Yet this is precisely where the idea for Rebecca's blow-dry brush kit, CurlME – the first product of her Pro Blo brand – came from.

A self-confessed "blow-dry addict", Rebecca spent most Saturday mornings in a salon getting her hair professionally dried and styled. "It wasn't the cheapest indulgence," she says, "but back then, I felt it was impossible to recreate a salon blow-dry at home. Not that I didn't try!

"One day, my ceramic brush broke. I clipped it into my fringe while drying the hair around it, hoping it would still produce the same result. It did – and that's where Pro Blo's story begins."

Rebecca then created CurlME – a detachable blow-dry brush kit. She felt other women would also want to save the time and expense of a salon visit if they could create the same results for themselves at home. "I think all women want to look and feel good, and having great hair is integral to this. Not everyone has the time to sit in a salon, or they may not have the disposable income to do so on a regular basis. I saw this as a real gap in the market, and I knew I could make Pro Blo into a luxurious yet affordable brand."

She invested her £20k savings into launching the business, which went into basic set-up costs and stock. "The cash ran dry very quickly," she recalls, "which meant early sales via the website were crucial if the business was to succeed past the start-up stage."

Rebecca experimented with different methods when it came to marketing her CurlME kit. She quickly found there was no right answer or magic route to sales. "It was a case of trial and error, and while some strategies worked, there were as many that fell flat. Over time, I learned that true marketing is much simpler than experts would have you believe: it's simply knowing who your customer is and where they can be found, and understanding why they'd buy your product. It doesn't matter what you're selling, as long as you know the answers to those questions.

"Social media has been at the centre of our marketing from the beginning, as well as being paramount to our growth. That said, we don't rely on it, as online algorithms change all the time, which can impact traffic to the website. We make sure we have a mix of online and offline campaigns running at any one time."

Rebecca used Instagram as one way to garner interest from customers. While this initially proved successful for the Pro Blo brand, she feels it became less synonymous with the platform and other similar 'Instabusinesses' once Selfridges came on to the scene. "They contacted us via an Instagram direct message around four months after we started out. I was so convinced that one of my friends was playing a prank on me that when they called the office to speak to me, I hung up on them! I'm still mortified about that. Luckily, it didn't put them off, and we had a proper CurlME launch at Selfridge's Trafford Centre branch. That was quite a moment."

As the product is predominantly sold online, Pro Blo's business model features low overheads as well as plenty of scope for new markets, both of which contribute to the company's growth. In 2017, Rebecca outsourced the company's warehousing facility, which further boosted Pro Blo's ability to scale up. Their products appeared in Harvey Nichols, ASOS and similar retail brands. Celebrities, bloggers and brand influencers whose online followers are hundreds of thousands across the globe have been keen to endorse and feature Pro Blo.

One of Rebecca's hurdles – certainly during the early days – was growing *too fast.* "Having money for stock that might sit with a retailer for nine months before we received a return has always presented a challenge. However, I always try to focus on what I can do about something rather than what I can't; instead of crying over a lack of cash, I focus on how to make more. It means I have to deal with everything in the moment, but I've got through tough times before, and doing so makes further issues less of a worry."

Rebecca also uses Quickbooks to help her keep on top of finances. "It's super-simple for someone like me who is not an accountant, and it allows me to monitor our cash flow any time of day, any day of the week."

Rebecca doesn't see herself as an entrepreneur, as the image she conjures up when imagining such a person is a high-flyer with a life of luxury. She says the reality, for her, is very different: "Despite the sleepless nights and the moments that make you question why you're in business, I honestly love what I do. Pro Blo isn't just a business; it's a part of me, a part of my life. I don't actually feel like I have a 'job'."

This was her driving force from day one: to make money from doing something she enjoyed. Her vision has shifted a little since then: she now measures the company's success by its reputation, and how much Pro Blo products are loved and respected within the beauty industry: "On a personal level, I work towards achieving balance in all areas of my life. There's a lot to be said for waking up every day and feeling excited about what lies ahead.

"Some people make good money as they head to the office every day, but few feel a real passion for what they do. The freedom to shape your life and the opportunities that come from running a business are not things money can buy."

Rebecca's favourite quote consists of rhetorical questions: "What if I fall? But, darling, what if you *fly*?" by Erin Hansen. She says, "I apply this to everything, because if you never take chances, how will you ever grow? I look back over the time I've been in business, and I know I've made many errors. But I had no real guidance, so it was inevitable.

"On the flipside, I honestly believe that had I been told all I know now, not only would I have not got to where I am, I would have probably run a mile. We learn more from our mistakes than our successes. I know that I'll always be a work in progress, but I'm okay with that."

Rebecca spends a lot of her time travelling, particularly to London as she is based in Liverpool. It's no surprise that her favourite days are those spent at the office. "I don't get to spend half as much time there as I'd like. I used to love travelling, but now I really appreciate routine and normality."

Rebecca's day begins at 5am. She initially checks her emails, although she often liaises with Pro Blo's clients in China, knowing that this time of day is much more convenient for them. She then heads to the beach with her dog for a brisk walk, which helps her to focus on what needs to be done that day. "I use this time as a form of meditation. A full hour with no phone contact, no social media, no emails to answer – just me, my pup and the beach.

"I get to the office around 8am and spend the morning in meetings or catching up with my operations manager. I see myself as hands-on, whereas my team would probably describe me as a control freak! I just want to be up to date with all aspects of the business." Lunch is usually spent with her social media manager, or with the head of marketing, discussing campaigns and concepts. Afternoons are no less busy. Then she heads home around 5pm.

Winding down after work can be a battle for anyone in today's always-switched-on world. How does she cope with this? "I'll admit, it is difficult to put your phone down when you can access your entire business on it. At the end of the day, it's a tangible object I can choose to put out of reach. And while I have experienced periods of stress and being overwhelmed, they don't last long."

It's clear that very little gets this girl down. And should Rebecca ever need a little pick-me-up that will make her look and feel a million dollars, we know just the thing ...

High:

"Two years in, we appeared at a trade show in London. Some friends had come to support me, which was a godsend, given that our stand was swamped the whole day.

"I remember filling a shelf with stock, and when I turned back again it was empty. I looked around and we were all dripping with sweat: we'd not stopped at any point during the eight hours. That was when I thought, 'Wow! We really have something here'. I'd like to say we went out afterwards and celebrated but, as soon as the show finished, all we wanted to do was crawl into our beds!"

Low:

"I don't have one, simply because I don't regret anything I've done or any decision I've made. They're not 'lows', they're lessons. What I will say is that there have been times when I should have trusted my gut. People with more experience and knowledge than me imparted advice that I (silently) disagreed with. I went through the motions anyway, even though I knew it was the wrong decision. As your confidence builds, you'll find this will happen less and less."

Golden nugget:

"My dad always says, 'Find something you love, and you'll never work a day in your life.' A wise man indeed!"

Advice to others:

"Remember what you wanted when you started out. It's so easy to become so consumed with hitting the next goal, then the next, that you forget just how far you've come. As a team, we acknowledge and celebrate every success. The little moments make the big ones, after all."

2
INNOVATING A NEW PRODUCT TO IMPROVE WOMEN'S HEALTH

Feel the fear and push through it.
Nothing ever happens if you stay in your comfort zone.

Tania Boler – Elvie

Innovation is what keeps everything moving forward and stops the world from standing still. While some entrepreneurs take an existing idea and do it better, slicker, cheaper or faster, there are as many who create products from scratch. This was the case for Tania, who used technology to greatly improve an issue mothers often struggle with.

Looking to regain control and strength in her pelvic floor area after the birth of her first child, Tania was keen to master the exercises the hospital recommended: "My Pilates instructor talked me through them, but when I tried to practise what she'd described at home, I had no idea if I was doing the exercises right or not, or if what I was doing was making any physical difference. I began to research pelvic floor health and that's when I saw a gap in the market."

Tania devised a solution that helps women strengthen their pelvic floor muscles; in doing so, she broke down taboos relating to women's health and encouraged conversations around the more intimate parts of their bodies.

Her first product was the award-winning Elvie Trainer, a Kegel trainer and app that makes exercising the pelvic floor muscles fun and is easy to use – anywhere, anytime. The device connects to an app that makes any movement of the muscles visual; it also guides the user through a short workout and tracks their progress over time.

"I delved into the world of women's health technology and found little innovation. The Elvie Trainer was just a starting point. I wanted to create a female-led company that makes useful products for women, by knowing exactly what problems they face – from pregnancy and childbirth to periods and menopause."

The success of the Elvie Trainer has been remarkable – it has since been recommended by more than a thousand healthcare professionals. Tania quickly achieved her aim of making it the smallest and smartest pelvic floor trainer on the market, and word of mouth pushed the majority of sales. She adds, "It was almost as if women had just been waiting for our product to come along. The marketing was organic, and we were proud to build an engaged community of women."

The popularity of the product helped Tania secure more than £8m in funding. This came from government grants and financing from external investors such as Google Maps co-founder Lars Rasmussen, ICAP founder Michael Spencer, Octopus Ventures and AllBright. Tania's team currently stands at around 40 employees, and the business is now on course to expand into 25 new territories.

Quick success meant that although the business was still in its start-up stages, it broke even within six months. An Elvie Trainer was featured in the nominees' goodie bags at the 2017 Oscars, and proved a hit with the celebs. Gwyneth Paltrow, January Jones and Khloé Kardashian are just some of the high-profile women to recommend the product. It has also been featured in numerous women's magazines, including *Vogue* and *Marie Claire.*

While it's great to receive such fantastic feedback, Tania is equally proud of the company's success at a grassroots level. She says, "We have recently secured an NHS Supply Chain obstetrics and gynaecology tender, which means women who are most in need receive an Elvie Trainer for free."

Creating category-defining, complex consumer electronics carries a lot of risks, however: "We produce the software components and the physical hardware, but we have to be absolutely certain the end product is not only high quality, but that everything is delivered within timeframes. No tech company wants to produce something that's inferior or to be seen lagging behind its core market."

Tania uses the technological creations of others to help Elvie Trainer run efficiently. For example, she uses the business communication platform Slack in the office: "The platform has significantly cut the number of internal emails we send, which makes my inbox much more manageable."

Tania describes her days as "pretty hectic". Her early mornings are typically filled with getting herself and her two small children ready for the day. She arrives at the office at 9am and initially spends time catching up with her various teams. The content of her working day differs according to her business-development priorities; lately, her focus has been on raising capital and growing and developing her workforce. As evening comes, she makes a concerted effort to balance work events with family life.

The one thing she finds difficult is switching off. Tania admits that her "mind is always racing". She regularly attends Barrecore classes – a form of exercise based on ballet and the barre. "I have to do something physically challenging before I'm mindful," she says.

So, how does Tania define success? "That's a really good question. When I started out, I just concentrated on creating a product that worked – one that solved the problem I was experiencing. From where I sit today, though, I think Elvie's greatest achievement is encouraging conversations that have been completely suppressed until now. My team and I take great pride from the fact we've helped women talk more freely about their bodies and their health."

Tania has a lot to be proud of – designing an innovative product, building a very successful business, creating a strong team, securing significant investment and improving female health. The fact she's helped many women share their worries and their experiences when they were previously too embarrassed to do so is simply the icing on the cake.

High:

"Winning my first government grant was the validation I needed that my idea had legs, that I wasn't crazy! I handed in my notice the very next day."

Low:

"We underestimated the role retailers play. Initially, we were reluctant to partner with Amazon, believing the platform to be a poor fit for the Elvie brand. It's now our key account."

Golden nugget:

"Have faith that you can do it, and don't think you won't be taken seriously because you're a woman. It can feel intimidating when you start out, but nowadays, there are more and more examples of successful women leading the way. There are a number of networks out there, within which are thousands of supportive female entrepreneurs."

Advice to others:

"You have to have some self-belief in your abilities and confidence in your idea; if you don't have these, you have to fake them until you do! You can project confidence – even if you're quaking in your boots underneath it all – such as speaking clearly and slowly, appearing relaxed and smiling. Your body language can mask your nerves if you apply a few simple tricks. Trying new things is the best way to build your confidence and skill set."

3
STARTING A BEAUTY BRAND IN YOUR RETIREMENT

Age is nothing but a number

Tricia Cusden – Look Fabulous Forever

There's no better proof that age is just a number than the story of Tricia Cusden, founder of Look Fabulous Forever. When she was launching her make-up range for older women after turning 65, Tricia not only found a new career, but she also hit on a real solution for ladies of a similar age who want to look as good as they feel.

Even with a shift in the attitude of numerous clothes designers who, over the past decade, have slowly learned to listen to women over 60 and include them in their ranges and designs, it appeared to Tricia that producers of make-up were still oblivious to the needs – and spending power –

of this section of the population. It was this lack of understanding from cosmetic companies and the indifference of young girls working on beauty counters that motivated Tricia to start her business. She says, "I got the feeling that the cosmetics industry wasn't really interested in me, unless they were selling their expensive anti-ageing creams. I wanted products that would flatter my features, not try and eradicate them. They seemed to know very little about an older woman's skin and their taste in cosmetics."

Despite having no experience of the cosmetics industry other than as a consumer, and although she based her business idea on assumptions about her market rather than actual research, Tricia went looking for a cosmetics manufacturer that would help her to create make-up specially formulated to suit the skin, eyes and lips of older women. Her plan was to sell the cosmetics directly through make-up parties in customers' homes; she subsequently trained as a make-up artist so she could demonstrate the products professionally.

However, the business had its own plans. The £40,000 savings Tricia had initially sunk into the business had been depleted by the time her products came to market. At first, she used YouTube – alongside other social media channels and platforms – to market the business, largely because it was free. But the channel soon proved to be the business's lifeline.

"I found a large group of like-minded women through YouTube, but the business's success – and, indeed, the effectiveness of all my content marketing – was down to the fact that I didn't sell to them. Instead, I gave make-up tips and advice, and brought real value to my subscribers, who then visited the Look Forever Fabulous website. They engaged with my brand because they liked what they saw, read and heard.

"I enjoy creating content – it's the best way to find potential customers I'd probably never get in front of without spending a lot of time, cost and effort. It creates a ripple effect, as one person likes your post and shares it with their friends, who then share it with the women they know, and so on."

Tricia continued to make more great decisions, one of which was bringing one of her daughters, a PR professional, on board, and tasking her with securing media coverage. Entering awards also brought accolades such as Google's Digital Achiever of the Year and Nectar's Entrepreneur of the Year.

Sales went stratospheric after Tricia appeared on BBC Breakfast. Following an initial injection of capital from an angel investor, it soon became clear the business needed more hands on deck than just Tricia and her family.

In 2016, the company's expansion saw Tricia welcome three more employees to the team. When the turnover of Look Fabulous Forever topped £2m the following year, further recruitment brought the team to 10 employees, and another round of angel investment ensured continued growth.

Building the business to such dizzy heights didn't come without its fair share of stresses and strains. Says Tricia, "Providing jobs is a fantastic thing to do, but with it comes great responsibility. You become accountable, and there's no question of the business failing when other people depend on it, which brings a certain level of pressure. Having to answer to investors also makes things very real."

Given the continued success of the company, it's clear these issues haven't caused Tricia serious grief – she is obviously well suited to the entrepreneurial way of life. "I love having autonomy and control over my working day. I think my natural drive and staying power help – entrepreneurs tend to be good at starting businesses, but many give up when things become tricky or mundane. I've put my heart and soul into Look Fabulous Forever, and I feel I'm now at a point where I can structure my time the way I want to. I'm lucky my daughters take control of the day-to-day business, which allows me to do the more exciting stuff – such as making media appearances."

As it is an online business, technology has been crucial to Look Fabulous Forever's success. "The quality of our systems, as part of the customer's overall experience, is critical. We've always understood the importance of this and continually invest in our software," explains Tricia. "In the early days, I constantly scrutinised the analytics and data, perhaps becoming a little too obsessed with the sales figures! Nowadays, other people maintain successful outcomes, and a sub-team ensures the business operates in the most efficient, cost-effective way.

"I don't just equate success with great sales figures – though of course they're important. I feel proud that I've created a wonderful, effective, hard-working team, and that I have acquired satisfied, loyal customers and happy investors, too. On a more personal level, being a spokesperson for older women on a range of issues and platforms is one achievement I didn't plan for, but one I truly enjoy and feel honoured to do.

"I love that no two days in the business are the same. I'm not a lark, I'm an owl, so having my own business means I can take my time in the mornings – I don't tend to function before 11am. I spend my days writing blog posts and other content, having meetings with the designers or members of my team, recording videos in the studio or being interviewed for a feature. I published a book recently, so I often do talks or appear on shows about that. Evenings tend to be when I catch up with answering my email and anything the team needs from me. I try to be in bed by 11.30pm and wind down before sleep by reading – I'm an avid reader.

"It's not that I don't feel stress – I've just learned to recognise and deal with it rather than just hoping it will go away. I have a personal trainer who visits twice a week, and I use my exercise bike – I've found that regular exercise definitely helps."

To quote Tricia's personal mantra, "It's never too late. Never too late to have a successful business, to have a happy life, to take control … to do anything." Tricia has shown that technology doesn't have to pass us by, and there's no reason why we can't start a second career when we're expected to put our feet up. She's also shown that having a good idea, a well-honed instinct and a never-give-up attitude can take you places.

High:

"There are many 'pinch me' moments in my journey; the most recent was having three of our primers in the goodie bags at the Oscars' ceremony. We had a fantastic time in Los Angeles, and it was such an honour – a testament to all our hard work."

Low:

"In the early days, I needed help to write a business plan for investors. Someone was recommended to me, but when that person and I started working together, I didn't feel they were the right fit. I tried to back out, but they persuaded me to continue, and the episode ended badly. I should have just listened to my gut from the beginning."

Golden nugget:

"Growth is what every new business wants, and although it's fantastic when it comes, you must make sure you can properly support it. Get the right people in at the right time – don't try and do everything yourself or cut corners. The business needs the right things in place or it won't fly."

Advice for others:

"If you can't find something out there in the market, it's likely other people are searching for it too. I was my own target market, and I just knew there was a lack of good make-up for women my age. Two beauty experts tried to tell me I was wrong, that it wouldn't work, and 'older women don't buy make-up'. Well, I certainly did! Don't wait for a gap in the market to become official – people don't always know what they want until they see it. If you believe there's some mileage in your idea, just go for it – it's never too late to have a successful business ... or to do anything."

4
REDUNDANCY WAS THE GATEWAY TO BEING A TECHNOLOGY ENTREPRENEUR

When one door shuts,
another one always opens

Leanne Bonner-Cooke MBE – e-bate limited

A career change was necessary for Leanne Bonner-Cooke when it came to following her passion. Through her background and training as an accountant, she found her experiences with the technological evolution of the early 1990s very interesting indeed. She realised early on that technology had the power to increase the efficiency of almost anything it was applied to.

This premise led her to launch her first company, Evolve – an award-winning provider of bespoke software products and solutions.

Leanne wanted to offer something different to the competitors sprouting up around her, who seemed more focused on creating tech than on whether the end products would actually improve their clients' businesses. This became her motivation: to make her clients' lives easier and make their businesses more cost-effective. Leanne and her team make it a priority to spend time with their clients throughout the process to ensure the technologies they create enable the business owner to achieve great things.

She says, "Businesses that launched around the same time as Evolve tended to under-quote to win contracts. Because they focused on 'creation' rather than 'solution', their clients had to pour more money into the projects further down the line. We've always sought clients with similar values to our own. We create an equal partnership that works towards one aim: creating an easy-to-use-and-apply solution at a realistic cost, under practical timelines."

Evolve's launch was self-funded. Leanne chose to take redundancy from her corporate role and used the small pot of money she received from the redundancy settlement to set up the business. She remembers sitting at her desk on day one when the reality of her decision began to sink in: "I'd rented an office and had buckets of positivity. Then it struck me: I'm alone! Oh my God, I need customers!" But luckily, Leanne's first client didn't take long to appear. This brought credence to the product she offered, and gave others an insight into what she could deliver.

Marketing a software business isn't easy, Leanne admits, especially when you can build almost anything and have long sales cycles. She found that the key to growing her customer base was getting "under the customer's skin", finding out their pain points, accurately assessing their needs and maximising all of the cross-selling opportunities once the clients were on board. She also cites the consistency of Evolve's branding and the leverage of her growing network as further components of the company's ongoing success.

In 2017, Leanne had another idea; to create product-based business and e-bate Limited was born. e-bate started as a team of rebate management specialists and software developers that spun out of Evolve. Our team specialised in building bespoke rebate solutions for companies that could not find a solution to fit their needs.

Rather than re-invent the wheel for each client, we recognised that there was a gap in the market for an intelligent rebate management solution that married end-to-end management with the clients' processes. In 2018, e-bate started trading: its purpose being to deliver a full end-to-end SaaS rebate management solution that offers a seamless user experience with intelligent tools to run your rebate program your way. e-bate brought along a whole new set of challenges for Leanne, "It was a new company and I wanted a new culture – that was challenging when you were moving across staff from one business to the other. But one thing I knew was that I wanted a team that was customer-centric, really believed in our vision and mission and were clear about how we could achieve it. In a start-up, the team needs to be agile as you are often wearing many hats."

The other challenge was seeking investment: Leanne realised that if she was going to get the product to market quickly there was a heavy investment required to build out the solution. With this in mind, Leanne started to network and build relationships with investors. She says, "This presented me with another challenge: I had never sought investment before and was surprised at how difficult it is. I am sure this is the case for everyone, but female-founded business only make up 6% of all VC money." However, she managed to close a round of £950K in July 2019 and another £950K in July 2020. This has allowed her to build the product, build out the team and go to market.

In 2020, Leanne sold Evolve so she could focus on e-bate Limited and ensure the company met its objectives.

There are many lessons that have been learned throughout Leanne's entrepreneurial journey. She says, "I had to stop being a control freak!" Being an employer is one thing, but who manages the manager? Leanne cites coaching as a tool that worked for her: "It can be lonely in business without an appropriate sounding board. My husband is wonderful at providing emotional support, but a coach helps me to get out of my own way, to eradicate any beliefs that are limiting."

Leanne is fully aware of how much she has learned during her entrepreneurial journey, from sales and marketing to building teams. "As businesses develop, success is measured in different ways. In Evolve, it was about turnover and profit and on the strength of our relationships with customers. In e-bate it is about Annual Recurring

Revenue and Customer Churn. You have to measure the things that are going to drive value in your business to ensure scalability."

So, given what Leanne has mastered over the course of time, is there anything she wishes she'd known before she started her entrepreneurial journey? "I wish I'd been more aware of the services offered by third parties – particularly how much they can cost and how little they sometimes deliver. For example, you can pay a marketing company hundreds of pounds to tell you what you already know, it's your product, your idea, you know the story better than anyone." She also wishes she'd acted on referrals from her network for the skills she needed to outsource.

Leanne tries to be "firm, fair and demanding" as an employer, a motto that has served her well. She survives on little sleep – through choice rather than worry – getting up at 6am for a refreshing walk through the countryside with her dog, followed by a gym session 3 times a week. She says, "Exercise is paramount to your mental health and wellbeing." She tucks into a good breakfast before starting her working day with a debrief with leadership team members. "It's important to me that we stay focused and organised as a team to get the essential stuff done."

As you'd expect from a busy business owner, no two days are the same. "I can be prepping and attending a board meeting, sitting in on strategy sessions for sales and marketing and product development or travelling to see a customer. Whatever the task, I have to be busy and I have to be having fun; I think that's the secret to a happy life at work. In the evenings, I typically catch up with friends and family or watch trash TV. At the weekends, I like to entertain as I love cooking different world cuisines, go for a bike ride or a longer dog walk. But normally I crash into bed around 10pm."

She firmly believes in a healthy balance between work and play – not just for herself, but for her team too. With the exception of Covid, Leanne likes her employees to enjoy team bonding and activities outside of work, from boat trips and fitness challenges to nights out. "When the weather looks good, my husband and I pack up the car and head off to the countryside with George our Cocker. We go for long, long walks and even longer drinking sessions in the local pub!"

High:

"Getting an MBE – what an honour! I was pleased and proud to learn I'd been nominated in the 2018 New Year's Honours list."

Low:

"Not trusting my instincts enough and letting things fester before making decisions, this is never good for the team."

Golden nugget:

"Go with your gut instinct – it's almost always right."

Advice to others:

"Regret the things you have done that have failed, rather than the things you never did."

5
BUILDING A BUSINESS SELLING TASTY MACARONS

What's for you won't go by you

Rachel Hanretty – Mademoiselle Macaron

From running a market stall to growing a fast-growing, multi-strand business, entrepreneur Rachel Hanretty's business has truly been built from the ground up. She launched Mademoiselle Macaron after spotting a gap in the market and soon became one of the first entrepreneurs to establish a strong brand with a product that went on to become a huge trend.

Rachel studied in Paris for her degree. While there, she became obsessed with the mouth-watering pastries and tasty macarons on offer. Back home in Scotland, she tried to hunt down some of the sweet delicacies she'd enjoyed in the

French capital. "Marks & Spencer had started to make macarons by then," she says, "but there were no high-quality examples from artisan producers. I'd tasted the real things: what I could get my hands on seemed like poor imitations by comparison."

While she worked to complete her studies, the idea of making and selling macarons herself grew and grew. She pitched the idea as part of a competition run by her university, and won £250. This sat in an account for a while as she created a brand, perfected various recipes and flavours for her macarons, and looked into suitable packaging solutions.

Initially, she traded from a market stall in the centre of Edinburgh. Despite it sounding like an uninspiring start, Rachel says it was great for brand engagement. "We had a colourful, eye-catching product that made people wander over and take a look. I would chat with them and share my passion for the humble macaron, as well as offer great customer service. People were inspired by this and became invested in my success, too. It also gave me the opportunity to experiment with different flavours and to find out what worked and what didn't."

As further proof of a demand for high-quality macarons, the stock on Rachel's stall sold out at every market she attended. She knew the time had come to take things further. "It was a huge step, opening a bricks-and-mortar store. I'd saved income from the stall and, together with the competition money and some inheritance, I opened Mademoiselle Macaron's shop and café. My loyal market-stall customers came with me, and my reputation spread by word of mouth.

"Opening the shop and having the kitchen space enabled me to scale up production and take on staff, which was a far cry from making macarons in my flat! Things continued to build, then eight months later, we were featured on James Martin's BBC show just before we launched online. By the time we sent out our first newsletter to announce the e-commerce site, we already had a large mailing list. Online sales now make up 40% of the business; it proved a real game-changer."

Publicity continued, and soon Rachel was approached by the likes of Harvey Nichols and five-star hotels that were interested in becoming wholesalers of her product. "To fulfil these opportunities, we needed to expand again, to gain more space for production. We could have worked into the night in the kitchen at the back of the shop if we had to meet demand, but it didn't make financial sense. We worked out that if we moved into a space that had more than one oven, we could increase production yet work fewer hours."

As well as scaling up to meet wholesaler demand, Rachel created new income streams, such as corporate gifts and wedding favours. Although these were profitable, resources were stretched, and new pressure points began to appear. Being both a manufacturer and a retailer meant it was doubly difficult to monitor costs and keep an eye on the production line. She adds, "When everything is made by hand, you can't cut corners or save time if you want to keep to the same high quality. Something as simple as a member of staff being off sick caused our output to go down and made the cost per macaron skyrocket. It also meant that any new variations or flavour developments had to be managed very, very carefully."

Incorporating Shopify and Xero made the business much more efficient. The e-commerce site handles all online sales and every transaction is automatically recorded in Xero. This gives Rachel accurate data at all times and saves hours of manual inputting. It also allows her to compare web sales against corporate and wedding orders, and to work out which expenses can be attributed to which part of the business.

Asana is a more recent technological solution that's already proving its worth – it's a project-management software that allows Rachel and her team to keep on top of wedding orders and plan campaigns around new flavours. Email marketing systems such as Omnisend also play a part, gathering data from Shopify sales for the company's e-marketing.

Although Rachel is still developing the various strands of the business, she has yet to extract herself from the overall enterprise. She's finding the journey of an entrepreneur often shapes itself: "I thought I'd be relentlessly hustling for the next stage of growth and planning multiple locations across the country, but the truth is, I have to be involved in the day-to-day business at the moment. And from what I thought being a business owner would entail, I thought I'd be a lot richer by now!

"I've come far enough, though, to know my perception of success has changed. Where it used to be selling out of everything on the market stall, it's less about volume nowadays and more about how we manage the cost of sales, as well as identifying missed opportunities – something we determine by monitoring our online conversion rates."

Does the stress and pressure ever get to her? "Sure! It's not that I ever thought it would be easy, but I didn't know I'd often feel lost, confused or simply exhausted. I wish someone would have told me that burnout is a real thing, and that if you don't take action, you risk losing passion for your business. My favourite saying is, 'What's for you won't go by you.' I'm a firm believer that the universe ultimately has your back."

And how does she organise? "It helps that I plan out my day the night before. When I get up, it's then easier to stick to schedule. I initially read my emails and look at our social media channels, then tackle the thing I least fancy doing before moving on with my day. Afterwards, I check in with the kitchen and shop and speak to brides about their bespoke orders. If I feel overwhelmed, I try to meditate, which can be hard to do in the midst of a busy kitchen or café. If this is the case, I go and do something manual, such as packing up web orders, which gives my brain the chance to calm down."

Rachel has certainly had a real taste of success. It'll be interesting to see what she plans to cook up in the future.

High:

"Winning the FL Summit Award for Scotland and the North East. I'd already won Young Entrepreneur of the Year, but this was different. There's something electric about being recognised by fellow businesspeople with no agenda other than to offer their support."

Low:

"There have been a few lows; most have been staff-related. One low point was when I split the retail side from the rest of the business. It needed its own focus, and I was already spread too thinly. I took on someone to manage the shop on a profit-sharing basis – the prototype for our first franchise. However, I underestimated the amount of time I needed to be involved. While I thought I'd offloaded and the decision would free up more of my time, it had the opposite effect, as I had to guide everything. It meant neither aspect of the business moved as far forward as it should have done." After a strategic decision, the café was closed to focus on where the growth is: online and wholesale.

Golden nugget:

"Your gut instinct will lead you to the right place."

Advice for others:

"Doing everything yourself saves pennies, which is fine at the beginning. But as soon as you have the money, pay someone else to do a task so that it's one less thing on your to-do list."

6
YOUR EMPLOYER CAN HELP YOU START UP

Don't underestimate your capabilities

Jo Stephenson – PHD Marketing

Making the leap from employee to business owner can be a scary prospect, but Jo Stephenson had the full backing of her employer when she jumped ship – along with the security that they'd be her first client.

Jo was working for the LINPAC Group when the company decided they needed to reduce costs significantly. She demonstrated to the board how much could be saved if they outsourced the marketing function to her as a third party and separate entity. They saw the benefits and long-term savings of such a move, and even paid a year's commission in advance so that Jo had the necessary funds to put a team together, and get resources and facilities in place. Soon after, PHD Marketing was born.

She says, "I'll forever be grateful to them for their faith in me. I knew that I was a good networker, and that once contacts knew I was no longer employed and was available to work for them, the phone would ring. I was right: six years later, we have 30 clients, 19 staff and a turnover above £1.5m – a figure that's not easy for service-based businesses to achieve."

What makes PHD Marketing different? "We specialise," she says. "We're a B2B marketing and strategy company that focuses on packaging sectors and life sciences sectors. We have competitors, but few understand what it's like to walk in clients' shoes. We don't need 'bedding in' time, and quickly understand what's relevant. To this day, we've never had to pitch for business – everything has come from recommendations.

"The key to gaining ground has been networking. We attend trade shows and join associations within relative industries; we're a familiar face at local networking groups, and we're always making new connections."

Because of her mortgage and similar financial demands, the cushion Jo's employer provided at the outset meant funding the business was never an issue. Still, Jo and two of her LINPAC colleagues who'd left the conglomerate to join her in the new venture worked out of hotel rooms for the first three months after starting the business. Eventually, the team found suitable office space, and the company really began to move. More team members were hired, which required some adjustments: "It felt odd, having strangers join us. We chose to hire 'will' over 'skill'; we can train anyone, but the right attitude is crucial."

Scaling the business was a challenge, particularly with a people-heavy business model that relies on technical knowledge and industry insight. "Once we'd honed our core values, we realised we had a proposition that could work in other markets."

PHD Marketing was recommended to a client in the electronics sector, and although this challenged the team, it proved the company could be just as successful in new market sectors. They subsequently secured clients in the chemical, distribution and life sciences industries. As a result of continued growth, the company split into two core teams: PR and digital. "I've always been very clear on what we do and what we don't do, based on our strengths. We consistently over-deliver; our high standards are everything to us."

Jo loves leading the business. She says she's often described as 'strong', though she prefers 'tenacious'. "'Strong' suggests a dominating nature and someone who can be insensitive, and that's not me at all. I'm a passionate, creative, energetic person who loves to motivate others. I'm a big believer in developing my team and investing in the future of the business. We recently hired two fantastic apprentices, and we've definitely benefited from their 'millennial thinking'. Good people management is a challenge, but when we grow, we add staff. We always need to be one step ahead of the growth curve. I think we're getting better at it."

Technology has been integral to the company's success. Jo invested heavily in Apple products to minimise virus risks and make connectivity simple. Microsoft Sharepoint has also had an impact; the file-sharing software allows members of the team to manage the constantly changing document versions. "Because we can see what each other is doing, it speeds up the approval process," says Jo. The team also uses a free app called Trello, which enables them to create client to-do lists and prioritise tasks. "It keeps everyone focused on key tasks and makes communication much smoother, especially now that we have offices in different locations."

Jo makes sure the whole team bonds. They often attend client events and formal dinners together, and socialise in their downtime. "I'm passionate about having a 'happy camp' back at base. Success in the early days meant keeping the clients we secured happy; today, I can't help but measure our success in growth (not necessarily profits) – however, having staff who are positive and feel fulfilled, as well as satisfied, loyal clients, is still absolutely paramount.

"I expected to feel pressure as a business owner, but I do laugh when people say, 'Oh, it must be lovely to not have a boss'. Who are they kidding?! Every single one of my clients is my boss; I have 30 of them demanding my time and attention!

"I wish I'd understood our value proposition much sooner. I spent too long comparing what we offered to what others were doing, and constantly worrying we weren't good enough. In actual fact, we were ahead of everyone – we just didn't know it!"

Jo believes in working hard and playing hard. "Why do it otherwise?" she says. She doesn't have a routine, and every day is different to the last. She spends a lot of time travelling to and from client meetings, and even her daily commute is a challenge. "It was a mistake to locate the business in the east when I live in the west!" she admits.

Back home, she's 'Mum' – a role that comes with its own to-do list. "My days are long and busy, but they're incredibly rewarding. I try to go out and get some fresh air when I need a break, and I love walking along the beach at weekends. My family helps me to de-stress."

Jo's plans for the business continue to push it forward: "It's important to maintain quality and sustain standards, but growth will come from moving into new markets."

It sounds like nothing and nowhere is off-limits – there's little doubt Jo's plans for further success will be realised, if PHD Marketing's present track record is anything to go by.

High:

"Winning a national award was a real moment for me. It felt as if all our hard work and achievements were finally being recognised. Sharing the success with my team meant the world.

"Another high point was taking on a client that turned over £2m; we'd been marketing their company for three years when they were sold for £54m. I should have taken a cut! Seriously, though, I felt so proud watching them fly as a result of the work we'd done. It was absolutely amazing."

Low:

"My commute, and the fact I travel so much, means I don't get to spend the amount of time with my team that I'd like. That's my biggest regret."

Golden nugget:

"Never approach your boss with a question – don't pass the monkey! Go to them with two solutions and ask them which they think is best. You can't flip your problems onto someone else; show that you've thought the situation through. My team knows my philosophy on this and I'm proud of how they take ownership of their work."

Advice for others:

"Have a great website – it's your shop window nowadays, and the first place a prospective client will look. Make sure it's up-to-date, dynamic and reflects your company's values. Put an 'A' team around you and trust your gut when it comes to people and deals – 99% of the time, if you think someone is lying, they are. Be open to advice and listen to others, and pay for the best when it comes to anything financial and legal. Lastly, don't underestimate your capabilities. As women, we tend to hold back, and our confidence can suffer. There are so many opportunities out there, you just need clarity, drive and commitment."

7
TURN YOUR PASSION FOR HELPING OTHERS INTO A RECRUITMENT BUSINESS

To achieve in life, you have to graft

Lucy Tootell – Temporis Legal Recruitment Ltd

Frustrated by the lack of client care in her job, Lucy Tootell knew there was a better way of doing things.

At the time, Lucy worked for a national recruiter, joining them while at university studying for her history degree. In the seven years she worked there, she progressed from resourcer to executive consultant, and was consistently billed as one of the top three in the company. However, while she was very good at her job, she didn't feel good about it.

Lucy says, "I loved the people part of my role and helping candidates into appropriate placements. However, my colleagues and many people in the legal recruitment industry were only focused on one thing – making their sale. I wanted to place more value on the candidate and client experiences, not rush them off the phone if the call was taking too long. The feedback I heard, in particular from candidates, over and over again, was that they felt like they were goods being traded. Relationship-building is at the heart of our industry, yet it didn't seem as if most agencies really got this.

"This helped me to recognise a gap in the market for a specialist recruitment agency that was completely focused on serving its clients. I didn't see making money as more important than building relationships. Though the field of recruitment is highly competitive, I knew that clients and candidates would use us again and again if we were fair and honest with them."

Together with her sister Rosie, Lucy launched Temporis Legal Recruitment Ltd. She approached the Small Firms' Guaranteed Loan Scheme, which loaned her £25k over three years to help her set up the company.

"I still remember how it felt to receive a cheque from our first paying customer! We'd worked so hard, putting in hour after hour, to make that first placement. Word of mouth built organically, and now, five years on, the business is still built on client testimonials and recommendations. We do use social media in our marketing, such as LinkedIn, Facebook, Twitter and Instagram, as well as blogging on our website, but it's our reputation that does the most work for us."

Just six months after launch, the sisters needed to move to a bigger office. "We'd worked in a tiny box room that had no air-conditioning, which made the summer days unbearably hot. Moving to an open-plan office that has a kitchen and seating area (and, most importantly, air-conditioning) in such a short time was a real indication that we were doing something right. We could meet clients and candidates on site too, which was another benefit."

The business grew quickly. Lucy cites the company's turnover of £1m in their second year as the next milestone. "This far exceeded our projections, and we exceeded them again in year three, when we turned over £1.5m. We're currently in the process of consolidating the business, which is yet another indication of how far we've come."

Lucy enjoys being in control of her own destiny and the responsibilities that come from being a business owner. "The buck stops with me as far as Temporis is concerned. We do have pressure points in the business, such as when a client doesn't pay within our timescales – or, in the most concerning cases, when they don't pay us at all. It's not just the hours worked that are lost, however – as we deal with permanent *and* temporary placements, we often payroll our candidates when they act as locums, subsequently invoicing our clients for the hours they work. We therefore need them to pay promptly so we're not left out of pocket. We'd rather turn down business than spend hours chasing late-paying clients – it's just not worth it."

The company's database is at the heart of the firm, and Lucy says they invested heavily in this software when the business launched. "The money we spent on our database has stood us in good stead as we've grown. It was a huge outlay at the beginning, but you have to speculate to accumulate, and that cost has been repaid many times over.

"Our business model is to promote from within. We give employees the tools to develop and progress their careers, so that they become successful consultants. This is why we only recruit at resourcer level – we prefer to train local talent ourselves. We see no ceiling to the potential that can be reached by women working in harmony. And we don't insist on graduates like some of our competitors do – so far, our staff retention rate is 100%."

That is indeed a real measure of success – but does it feel as if there are still mountains to climb? "When we first started the business, I measured success financially, and while this hasn't changed, I'm just as proud we've created a business that is respected within its industry. I am proud our service is so good that clients and candidates are happy to recommend us again and again.

"It was scary, leaving an established position to launch Temporis. I wish I'd not worried so much that it would all work out. Stepping into the unknown can be paralysing, especially for a natural-born worrier like me! I suffered quite a few sleepless nights in the beginning; looking back, I wish I'd been easier on myself and trusted my abilities."

Lucy describes another situation that turned into a learning curve, and delivered the lesson that trust is hard-earned and easily lost. "Initially, I was keen to believe everyone is fair in business, just as I am. When one of our largest clients went into administration, they owed Temporis £40k. This didn't cause us huge financial difficulties because of the way I led the business, however I believed them when they repeatedly told us we would be paid. I continued sending – and payrolling – a large number of locums. They knew full well that they wouldn't be able to pay our invoices, yet they allowed us to continue."

Her favourite quote is from Winston Churchill, who said, "Success is not final, failure is not fatal; it is the courage to continue that counts". Lucy saw this quote around the time she launched the business, and it resonated with her so much that it became the company's motto – it's even written in large letters on the office wall.

"Success isn't final in business. You can't rest on your laurels, pat yourself on the back and take your foot off the pedal. You always have to think about what's next. Even more crucial is how you deal with failure. You can't win everything; you have to make mistakes to learn. And courage … well, you definitely need that. Running a business is hard – no matter what happens, however great a blow you've been dealt, or how overwhelming it may all seem, you have to soldier on. You can't give up."

As a mum to a 4 year old and a 2 year old Lucy has little time to rest when she gets home. "My daily routine means wearing many different hats, depending on what time of day it is. I begin the day around 6.30am with a coffee and CBeebies! Once I've got my little boy dressed, my husband takes over so I can shower, get ready for work and check my emails. My husband and I are incredibly lucky in that our parents share childcare. This, along with the one day a week my son spends at nursery, means I can really focus on work when I'm there.

"I head into the office at 8am, where I have another coffee and breakfast. An average day consists of me speaking with candidates about roles, and with clients about their requirements. I arrange interviews and book locum cover, then address my managerial responsibilities – like conducting monthly reviews with my consultants, overseeing internal recruitment, liaising with external providers, etc. I'll never not fee-earn; I thrive on the buzz of recruitment. I have to be on the sales floor with my colleagues or I'd go stir crazy!

"I leave the office around 5.30pm to pick my little boy up. I do his bath and bed routine, except on Mondays when I play tennis in a competitive league. Tennis is my outlet. It's a fantastic way to forget the stresses of the day and just focus on me for a couple of hours."

Lucy admits to struggling with stress and anxiety from time to time: "Stress management is something I need to do on a daily basis." She was signed off work from stress before starting the company, which was when she realised things needed to change. It was this decision that led her to launch Temporis.

Says Lucy, "Owning and running your own business is stressful. Recruitment is a target-driven environment. The two together can be a lot to manage. I have regular hypnotherapy, which really helps. I was always one of those people who was dubious of alternative therapies, but four months down the line, I swear by it. I also practise mindfulness every day and keep a gratitude journal, which helps me to recognise the good things, however small.

"If I was to describe myself, I'd say I was a typical working mother who has many responsibilities and who juggles the day away. My life is hectic, but I'm very happy."

High:

"Winning an 'FL Women of the Year' award for North East, Yorkshire and Scotland. I didn't even expect to be nominated, let alone win. Being at the ceremony with Rosie was such a 'pinch me' moment. I was so overwhelmed when they called my name that when I went to collect my award, I almost fell over. Given that I was eight months pregnant, it had everyone gasping! But the recognition meant all our blood, sweat and tears had been worthwhile."

Low:

"The situation I mentioned, concerning the client who knew they didn't have the money to pay us but who let us continue, was definitely a valuable lesson to learn. It isn't one I regret, though. From this situation, I learned not to let pride stand in the way of important business decisions. After they went into administration, we had numerous difficult conversations with the new owners. Most people would have walked away, but what would that have achieved? I made the decision to work with them, as long as it was on our terms. That client is still with us today."

Golden nugget:

"My parents drilled into me that if you've done your best, that's all you can ask. My own nugget is that of course it's hard – if it was easy, everyone would do it! As Churchill said, 'Success is not final, failure is not fatal; it is the courage to continue that counts.'"

Advice for others:

"Others may do things that seem at odds to how you do them. Don't be tempted to follow them – instead, be true to yourself. Don't try and be something you're not. Focus on what you want your brand to say, how you want to be perceived and what you want people to recognise you for."

8
A GLOBAL MEET-AND-ASSIST SERVICE

Tough times don't last forever – tough girls do

Christina Lawford – DiamondAir

After starting her entrepreneurial journey aged 13, Christina was always destined to have her own business. She and her classmates were encouraged to launch their own businesses as part of a school project. At the time, a friend's mum worked for the company that had taken over The Body Shop's original factory and begun to make similar products. Christina did a deal with them and bought some of their stock at a good price. When she began to sell her wares to friends and teachers at school, she made such a profit that the headmaster called her into his office, concerned that the school was missing out on good money!

Her first enterprise may have been limiting, but as she says, "Being an entrepreneur is not something you set out to do, it's something you *are*." Fast forward to today, and Christina, perhaps unsurprisingly, now has a multi-million-pound turnover business: DiamondAir. The company provides bespoke meet-and-assist services within 600 airports and train stations across the globe, regardless of cabin class or provider/carrier. They also offer a top-tier service in more than 50 airports, known as 'Airport by Invitation'. The company is recognised as the Global Market Leader of Premium Airport Services by the travel industry.

It wasn't necessarily the company Christina always planned to launch; if anything, she describes it as "something she fell into". She was working for Sky Diamond at Heathrow Airport round the clock, seven days a week. Her role involved greeting customers and helping them at check-in, issuing tickets and sorting their seats. She says, "As I spent so much time at Heathrow, I could see how many issues celebrities and business travellers experienced as they tried to get through one of the world's busiest airports. I began to approach groups and music artists, showing the tour managers how I could be of help. Once they realised how much time and stress I could save them, they recommended me to their travel agents.

"Things just went from there. DiamondAir evolved from Sky Diamond and was completely demand-driven. At the time, no one was delivering an airside service. Having the appropriate security clearance was critical – my international competitors were all airside, and I used their model to convince Heathrow to give us an airside licence. It took 10 years, but eventually, they did."

Having an international network paid dividends, too. "If the client needed assistance in another airport, I would find someone who could help them – I would never let them down. Though some airlines claimed to offer a complimentary service to their top-tier passengers, it wasn't consistent, and they could never meet true demand. DiamondAir was independent of any airline and something people could pay for whenever they needed it."

Because the business evolved, funding wasn't needed in the early days. However, as it expanded, investment has been necessary at times. The business's bank, HSBC, has always offered its support in this area, which is why Christina is still with them 20 years later.

Her personal recommendation is DiamondAir's most effective route to new customers. "Growth, however, has come from a number of things: winning the American Express Centurion global contract; becoming the first ever meet-and-assist company for Eurostar (with full security access!); and building a strong, capable management team – this has really helped take the company to the next level."

Christina confesses that the company has also had its fair share of growing pains: "Transitioning to a volume model while committing to deliver a VIP bespoke service to every client was definitely a challenge. DiamondAir's story does not tell of an overnight success – it's more a slow burner that has had to deal with every setback organically and strategically. For example, celebrities can be demanding and allow no room for error. We therefore have systems in place to ensure confidentiality and consistency, as well as a team that's experienced and equipped to handle any hiccup. We've learned that things can and will go wrong, but your reputation stands on how you handle a situation.

"It's not easy delivering a service that's 24 hours a day, seven days a week, which is why we invest so much in our team – they're our biggest and best asset. Airport licences and regulations regularly change, which could impact the business. We have a wonderful legal and compliance specialist who oversees such things, and who keeps us up to speed. Finance also presents a continual challenge; we have a highly capable financial controller who manages our accounts and offers advice whenever we need it."

Salesforce underpins the business's booking system. Its capability to integrate with their clients' systems has created numerous opportunities and increased sales. Having a number of other technologies and software solutions has helped make the business paperless, scalable and efficient.

Does she have any regrets? "Looking back, I wish I'd taken an accountancy course during the early days of the business. I also wish I'd paid more attention to the small print in every document, particularly those concerning my directorship."

Christina describes herself as a "contradiction", in that she's outwardly confident but can sometimes suffer from low self-esteem. "I don't care what people think of me; I care for others more than myself. I am fear*less* in business, but also fear*ful* that I won't succeed."

As for routine, the only thing that tends to be the same, day in, day out, is Christina's approach. She *decides* to have a great day, seeing it as a choice rather than a reaction. She feels blessed to have the life she has and she strives to remain permanently positive. "Exercise and the occasional glass of wine certainly help in this regard though!" she laughs.

High:

"Oh, I have many highs. Winning my first big contract with a company called Globepost when I was 19, then winning the Kuoni contract a year later. I've dealt with 90% of the UK music industry and 80% of the US music scene. I have met and looked after everyone, and become a close friend and ally to musicians such as Lionel Richie and The Spice Girls – I was even known as 'Airport Spice' at one time! Watching airlines that initially tried to block DiamondAir changing their mind and wanting to work with us.

"I remember how it felt when the business passed £3m in sales, and also when it passed £5m. Ultimately, though, I don't think I've had my 'highest high' yet. There's so much more I'd like to achieve."

Low:

"People trying to take control of the business from me as part of a shareholder dispute. It's settled and done with now, and I still hold 100% of the business, but it was a stressful, demoralising experience. Ex-employees have taken intellectual property from the company, and competition has threatened to steal our position. However, it helped to see these situations as distractions rather than my true focus – as a result, they didn't consume me. I received a *lot* of support from my fantastic lawyer, and from my friends, family and mentors, which I'm incredibly thankful for. I know I wouldn't be the person I am today if I hadn't gone through these experiences."

As of 2021, the biggest challenge I have ever experienced must be the pandemic. DiamondAir was decimated during the pandemic. In March 2020 Covid threw a grenade into our business. We went from circa 60,000 VIP movements a year to seeing just 14 bookings in the entire month of April 2020. It broke my heart and every part of me to watch the business I had built evaporate. BUT I didn't give up: we pivoted into COVID testing at the airport and are now deemed the Concierge service for COVID testing; we even offer a 2-hour turn around for PCR test results and offer a nurse home visit service for high net worth and high profile clients. It saved us and although I sadly lost nearly 50% of my staff (some of whom have worked for me for over 20 years), I managed to retain 43 jobs. I have lost so much but learnt so much about myself and how resilient you can be when everything is threatened. We are not out of the woods yet, but I know we will emerge stronger and better for it. Oh, I also signed our biggest agreement in lockdown. We are now on BA.com as their global meet and assist company. I just thought I would give you our COVID overview as it seemed so relevant to my story and prevalent to businesses now.

Golden nugget:

"Revenue is vanity, profit is sanity and cash is reality" Remember that everything is a potential opportunity. It's also a numbers game: the more you put in, the more you will get out."

Advice to others:

"Protect what you build, and do not take on a shareholder without thorough due diligence and background checks. Psychopaths can wear suits! Believe in yourself. Remember: you're *amazing*. Don't listen to the naysayers – and never, ever give up. Remember to take time off – time off is an investment in future performance. Take it and give it: remember to be kind to yourself."

9
TURNING YOUR PASSION FOR HELPING OTHERS INTO A MULTIMILLION-POUND BUSINESS

Don't sweat the small stuff

Sally Fielding – Sally's Cottages

In her own words, Sally Fielding's multimillion-pound business "came about by accident". Although her company, Sally's Cottages – a holiday lettings agency with 570 properties throughout the Lake District and Cumbria – wasn't what she had originally planned to do with her time, she has still worked very, very hard to get it where it is today.

Chatting with her next-door neighbour one day, Sally came up with what she thought was a simple solution to her neighbour's worries. She says, "My neighbour was upset because she wanted to let her cottage out on a long-term basis, but couldn't find anyone that was interested. I said, 'I tell you what, Di, why don't I rent it from you and sub-let it?' I rented it from her for £500 a month and sub-let it for £500 per week."

Sally soon realised she had the skills needed to maximise the visibility of her neighbour's cottage. "I already had a business designing websites, and this was at the time when the internet was just emerging. I set up a website for the cottage and placed an advert with a few online directories; before long, the property was fully booked, week in, week out."

Word of Sally's success spread to other residents of her small village, and those who also had holiday homes approached her to do the same for them. "I launched Sally's Cottages and acted as a letting agency. I didn't own or rent the cottages I took on, I just advertised and promoted them on behalf of the owners, charging a commission for every booking I took. This is still how we operate today, although we also offer a managed service where we organise the cleaning of the property after it's been used and take care of any routine maintenance."

When Sally's portfolio reached 30 cottages she realised the business was at a tipping point. She sat down with her husband, Rob, and debated whether to keep the business small – and therefore manageable between the two of them – or if they should take the next steps towards growing the company as far as they could.

While the smell of success was clearly enticing, it wasn't an easy road ahead. Sally says, "We could already see that it was becoming more difficult to get a brand seen on the internet, and that more funds would be required to break away from our competitors. It was a good time to grow – if we'd decided to keep the business at 30 properties, I doubt we'd even exist today."

The couple worked hard to remain visible online. They took time to understand what their brand values and proposition were – although it may seem obvious as a week/weekend in a holiday cottage, Sally and Rob knew it was more than that. Their offering wasn't tangible when they were asking customers to part with their money. Instead, they had to sell an ideal. A dream. An experience … An escape from everyday life. "We believe in those little moments of happiness, and this comes through in all our marketing, online and offline."

Their approach works: Sally's Cottages took bookings to the value of £8m in 2019.

Growing the business also meant taking on another person. Sally cites this as "a revelation". "When there were more emails at 10pm than there had been at 8am, we knew it was time for more hands on deck. It proved one of the best decisions we've ever made, and all of a sudden there were enough hours in the day to get everything done."

Realising that no other holiday cottage lettings agency had the means to take online bookings gave the couple the opportunity to lead the pack. As there was no off-the-peg solution for the business's needs, Sally hired a coder and designer, who developed a system that's still going strong today – even though the company now has 540 cottages to cope with on a daily basis.

Growth was also responsible for the move into "proper offices", which overhauled the way the team worked. She says, "I hadn't realised how tiring it was having people work from our house from 9am to 9pm, seven days a week. Once we moved to offices in Keswick, I finally saw the importance of switching off now and again. We felt more professional, and looked it, too – even though we were doing the same things we'd done for years. People's perceptions of us changed and we grew quickly – you could say that having our office was the equivalent of a very expensive advert!"

Word of mouth has always proved Sally's Cottages' most effective marketing initiative. Sally believes this slow rise to success brought manageable growth and helped the team to fulfil their promises, which only served to reinforce the quality of their brand. "It also meant we were able to make mistakes and learn from them, as the stakes were relatively low," she adds.

Sally confesses she gets bored easily and any plans she makes are open to change. "I like to get on with things, then tweak later if need be. If I have a thought or idea, I don't need reams of paper, fancy software, or hours and hours to plan it out – five minutes and the back of an envelope will do! I find that if I don't act on something when it pops in my head, it probably won't happen."

Isn't that a trait of an entrepreneur – being a doer rather than a thinker? "I'm always loathe to call myself an entrepreneur as having a holiday cottage lettings agency is nothing new. That said, some of the things we do within the business are wonderfully creative; for example, I took my desk to the top of Blencathra for a photo shoot."

Being one of the most prominent brands in its sector was achievable when the internet was young, but now, the bigger agencies have more funds behind them which they use to pay for advertising on Google. Instead of relying on Google advertising, Sally decided to develop the brand of Sally's Cottages instead, to become a recognised and trusted name. This meant being creative and agile. It meant getting up at 4am for a photo shoot. It meant answering Facebook comments at midnight. It meant they could stay one step ahead. That hasn't stopped them from piggy-backing on her brand, though.

Does it ever get too much? "It has its moments, though I love getting up every day and doing what I do. My parents had their own business, so I always knew it required long hours. People see the fun side of having a business and assume that, as the owner, you can take time off whenever you like. It's actually only now that I can have the occasional day off.

"In the beginning, I did everything. If I went out, I'd divert the phone to my mobile. If it rang, I answered it. My friends hated this, but I knew that if I didn't answer the phone, whoever was on the other end would call the next agency and book with them instead. And I only took two days off when my first two children were born, because we didn't have any employees at that point. The babies slept in a basket by my desk, or they were strapped to my chest as I answered emails!"

Sally walks four miles every day, which she says helps her maintain perspective as well as keeping her fit. She believes success has always been about maximising bookings and ensuring guests have a great time. "That never changes." While she enjoys what she's achieved, there are things she would change if she could do it all again. "I don't believe we've made any huge mistakes, I just wish we'd scaled the business sooner than we did. I should have taken someone on earlier instead of trying to do everything myself.

"Nowadays, I'm heavily involved in the marketing side of the business, though I move around according to what needs me. Rob and I continue to discuss the future of the company on a regular basis, and we've been working on a bespoke system for the past 18 months, which has taken a lot of our focus and energy to get right."

Sally's usually at her desk for 8.15am each morning, working until 4.30pm, which is when she picks the kids up from school. When they're in bed, she often does another couple of hours' work. Finally, she switches off completely with a good book. "There's nothing like escaping to another world," she laughs. "It's wonderful." No doubt the thousands of guests in her numerous cottages agree.

High:

"Playing a part in someone else's success. Suzanna was one of our longest-serving employees before she left us to set up wild-swimming tours in the Lake District. Every time she gets a mention in a magazine or a newspaper, she emails me; it's great to think that she joined us, learned from us and used those skills to create another great business.

"Also, winning our first award was a real high point. When you're running your own business, there's no one to say 'Well done, you've done a great job today', and it can therefore be hard to maintain your confidence. That award gave us a tremendous boost – it was effectively someone else saying exactly that."

Low:

"Perhaps my biggest regret is missed opportunities. There have been so many ideas that haven't come to fruition simply because we were too busy to lend our time to them, or because we deemed them too risky."

Golden nugget:

"I'm not the best at thinking on my feet. Someone once said to me: If you have a difficult message to give, come up with three sentences you can say over and over again, regardless of what's being said to you. It's powerful and it really works."

Advice for others:

"Get rid of your television. It's amazing what else you can do – what you can achieve – with the hours you'd otherwise waste staring at the screen!"

Exiting the business:

Sally's Cottages was sold to Travel Chapter in 2021. We kept going through the pandemic and managed to get our costs down (we cut marketing by 90% for example) but costs were still £80k per month. Fortunately, we'd been advised years ago to save enough to keep going for a year for just in case the music stopped. I'm so glad that we did as we had 9 months of zero income.

However, it had taken years to save those funds and we're now in a position where if there were more lockdowns or if the music stopped in a different way, we'd struggle. So we took the decision to sell. Fortunately, with the brand being so strong we had no shortage of people who were interested in buying. We chose a company that was smaller and who had similar values to us. They intend to keep the business running as it already does, with everyone continuing to do the job that they already do. And they have the funds behind them to put into marketing for next year which will be good for all our cottage owners.

GOLDEN RULES FOR START-UPS

There's no time limit on success

The start-up phase is one of the most challenging stages in an entrepreneur's life because the learning curve is steep, and the sheer volume of things that you need to put in place to begin trading and delivering value to your customers can be overwhelming. You will soon find yourself burning the candle at both ends just to bring your idea into fruition. So, it is especially important that you build a solid foundation and habits that can see you through the journey.

Here is a summary of the top tips from the unstoppable women we've met so far for those still in their business start-up phase.

1. Marketing is fundamental

Over time, you will learn that true marketing is much simpler than experts would have you believe. It is simply knowing who your customer is and where they can be found and understanding why they would buy your product. Leverage digital media but do not rely too heavily on it as online algorithms change all the time, which can impact the results you get over time. Learn how to market your business because at the start of the journey you will probably be the most knowledgeable and passionate about it.

2. Stay with the why

Remember what you wanted to achieve when you took the leap of faith to start your business. It is easy to become so consumed with hitting the next goal, then the next, that you forget just how far you have come. Get into the habit of celebrating the small as well as big wins. The journey is more important than the destination. It is after all, the little moments that make the big ones.

3. Value Your time

Make time in your life for your business and your family. Set healthy boundaries for work and rest and be vigilant of distractions. For example, get rid of distractions like social media apps if you find yourself mindlessly wasting time on them. You will be amazed what you can achieve – with the hours you would otherwise waste staring and mindlessly scrolling through screens.

4. Believe in yourself

Self-doubt is a mental game we all must deal with, but you must remind yourself of all the barriers and obstacles you had to overcome to get where you are today. Use past successes to coach yourself into believing in your abilities. Get into the habit of trusting that everything always works out – even the darkest moments do not last forever. Do not listen to the naysayers as their negativity can feed your self-doubt. Surround yourself with people who can be kind yet honest when you need it. Also, remember that there is no time limit on success – take your time if you need to. Have faith, visualise your end goal, and be kind to people, especially yourself.

5. Protect what you build

Do not take on a shareholder without thorough due diligence and background checks. Psychopaths can wear suits! It is likely that those closest to you will be the ones to take advantage, sadly, so always err on the side of caution when it comes to giving away what you have built.

6. Stay true to yourself

Others may do things that seem to work but are at odds with your values. Do not be tempted to follow them – instead, be true to yourself. Do not try and be something you are not. Focus on what you want your brand to say, how you want to be perceived and what you want people to recognise you for. Remind yourself that a flower does not think of competing with the flower next to it, it just blooms.

7. Go digital

The entire world is now online. The internet is not optional. It is your shop window and the first place a prospective client will search for. Make sure your online presence or profile is up-to-date, dynamic and reflects you and your company's values. Leverage social media to connect with your potential clients and customers at less cost than advertising.

8. Build a team

Start building your dream team as soon as you able to. You do not always have to employ people to start building your team. Focus on finding freelancers, suppliers and eventually employees who fit the culture and respect the values of your company. Surround yourself with 'A-class' team players and trust your gut when it comes to people and deals. 99% of the time, if you think someone is not a fit, they will not be. Finding the right people takes time and money, so be ready to pay for the best – especially when it comes to anything financial and legal related.

9. Commit – it is a marathon not a sprint

Most of us hold back due to the fear of failure or judgement. We are afraid to put our whole self forward and to push our businesses because we do not want to be seen as pushy or bossy. People will always judge you no matter what you do. Don't let the fear of judgement keep you from committing fully to your business. Being in business is like being married to your business or having another child. It needs your full attention and energy, and you need to be committed and ready to give it what it needs so it can grow and give you the freedom that you so deserve.

10. Delegate

Doing everything yourself is impractical. It saves pennies. As soon as you can afford to pay someone to ease the workload so you can have the energy and headspace to focus on strategic plans. When you delegate, acknowledge the contribution that others have made to your success and show your gratitude. It is a team effort.

11. Trust your instincts

You must have overcome your initial fears to start your business. You need to keep persevering despite the presence of fear. Create the space – both physically and mentally – for you to get in touch with instinct so you can trust your gut. That inner intuition will rarely let you down.

12. Get the right processes and systems in place

Growth is what every new business wants, and although it is fantastic when it comes, you must make sure you can properly support it and control the pace of growth. Using the right technology from day one will make your business scalable. Invest in the right systems and create the right workflows and processes that can be repeated and are easy to delegate.

SECTION 2: SCALING UP

It takes a lot of grit to get there

According to research by Ernst & Young, 30% of businesses in the US are owned by women, but only 2% of these businesses break the $1m revenue mark. The research goes on to show that businesses owned by men are 3.5 times more likely to reach the million-dollar revenue mark than those owned by women. We know there are a many complex challenges facing women entrepreneurs when it comes to sustaining and scaling their businesses, but two of the most prominent contributing factors are that: 1) women are still largely responsible for the caring responsibilities in their families; and 2) only 3% of investment goes to businesses run by women, despite statistics proving that women significantly outperform men in business.

Yet despite the fact the cards seem really stacked up against female entrepreneurs, we have witnessed extraordinary demonstrations of strength, resilience and creativity from our female founders. Remember, these are women just like you, who chose to be unstoppable despite the normal challenges they face.

I heard Dame Stephanie Shirley sharing this quote about running her business: "If it were easy, we would all be millionaires. If it is a surprise that someone like me should be a commercial success, it is simply because other people have done it for me. It was 25 years before we paid a dividend. It was a slow burn. People talk about my overnight success, but 25 years is a long time to stick to something before it actually comes good."

What she said really resonated with me because it is the halfway point, the middle of any race or marathon, that is the toughest place to be. Do you carry on running the race, or do you give up? When everybody else looks like they are making a success of their lives and their businesses, and you are faced with seemingly unsurmountable daily challenges, how do you stay motivated so you can be the leader the business needs to move it to the next level? Are some people naturally gifted, born leaders and visionaries, or can we all learn to be better entrepreneurs and leaders? What do you do when the stats are stacked up against you?

I was fascinated to learn while reading Angela Duckworth's best-selling book *Grit: The Power of Passion and Persistence* that natural talent can only take you so far – ultimately, it is your grit and ability to stay focused over really long periods of time that eventually lead to your success. I recommend reading her book and also taking the Grit Test found on her website, https://angeladuckworth.com/grit-scale/.

The Grit Test is a set of ten questions that will help you understand and gain further insight on how passionate and persevering you are compared to others. In her book, Duckworth mentions the research conducted by Chia-Jung Tsay, which explores investors' preferences for people either perceived as natural entrepreneurs or as hard workers – aka "strivers". The research proved that investors, like the public, tend to have a bias towards perceived natural talent, which is not always the best indicator of success. According to Duckworth's research, grit is a truer indicator of success. The entrepreneurs who carry on running their businesses long after others have given up are those who have grit. Having this single characteristic gives us mere mortals hope that by holding on we all can achieve greater things than we ever imagined possible based on our so-called natural born talents.

10
BUILDING A DIGITAL PLATFORM, ONE SUBSCRIPTION AT A TIME

Your network is your net worth

Susanna Lawson – OneFile

"Am I an entrepreneur? Or just someone who owns a business?" Years after she launched OneFile, this was the question Susanna Lawson still found difficult to answer.

Clearly, she's an entrepreneur – albeit a very modest one. Susanna knew first-hand that there was a gap in the market for OneFile, which provides cloud-based software that helps assess and support in-house training, apprenticeships and vocational courses. Together with her partner, Chris, Susanna created OneFile and turned it into the successful organisation it is today: a company that employs 84 people and supports almost 1.3 million users worldwide.

The idea for the business arose from Susanna's realisation that there had to be a better way of doing things. Often travelling long distances to deliver training, she only saw a brief snapshot of an individual's development; the limited time she spent physically with apprentices and employees made it difficult to be truly objective about their overall progress. Moving the process online not only made things easier, it also proved more cost-effective. Progress was easier to audit when cloud-based as evidence could more easily be uploaded; it also gave specialist assessors the opportunity to access users' portfolios, which ultimately improved the quality of the training.

Susanna believes word of mouth was the company's most effective strategy for continual sales. Once potential customers heard about the software and understood how it could solve many of their problems, it practically sold itself. But even with a much-needed solution to offer, Susanna knew outstanding customer service was what made her brand memorable. She says, "It would be easy to make shortcuts, but what's the point of spending time winning someone's business if you over-sell and under-deliver? The customer will simply leave as soon as they can."

Large corporations, the public sector and educational organisations snapped up OneFile in droves. Growth came organically, thanks to both hard work and maximising every opportunity. Susanna and Chris initially grew the business without third-party investment or debts, preferring instead to roll profit back into the business to support its expansion. As the business grew, they have embraced investments and are currently in the process of raising investment to support their next growth phase.

A turning point came two years after the software launched: "At this point, we were still putting in long, long days from our back bedroom. We knew we had to bite the bullet and hire our first employee, but to do that, we needed an office for us all to work from. This was a gigantic step for us. It felt like OneFile was a 'proper' business and our mindset changed: we were not just having to travel to work, we were now also responsible for someone else."

Endorsements came from influential and relevant boards and organisations. Susanna says the feedback boosted their confidence: "It seemed to prove we were doing everything right."

As the business expanded, Susanna and Chris put structures and processes in place to support growth. They were also savvy enough to hire people with skills in specific areas, such as marketing, technical support, software development and sales. "By splitting the business into areas, we could identify where we needed further resources. We realised it wasn't good for the business for me and Chris to try and do a bit of everything – we needed to let the experts do what they were good at."

That's not to say things always went to plan. Says Susanna, "There are some stages of growth where it feels like things are going backwards. When we had around 25 employees, problems surfaced, and once again, there were problems when the team swelled to 50 members of staff.

The first time, I couldn't understand exactly why cracks were beginning to show – everything seemed to be going well enough, and all the correct processes were in place." However as however as the business grew, the processes or the expertise of the team were not able to cope with rapid growth.

Nowadays, she admits she's much better at spotting what she describes as "growing pains". She also concedes that she didn't deal with the business's shakier moments very well to begin with, perhaps only taking on board what the relevant issues were after they'd already been resolved and the problems were well behind them.

Susanna cites OneFile's Customer Relationship Management (CRM) system as a significant contributor to its success, calling it "a revelation". Once the business began to attract a number of opportunities, warm leads and actual sales, spreadsheets and simple databases were no longer sufficient. "The whole process became much easier with the CRM, which meant all aspects of the pipeline were visible. Initiatives became measurable, and actions became accountable."

Success for Susanna has evolved as much as the business. At the outset, her focus was on sales; now, Susanna measures successes by the company's reputation. "It's incredibly satisfying to know that the sector we work in speaks highly of us – not just of our product, but of our approach, our standards of care and our ethics, too."

Even though ongoing development and knowledge is important to Susanna, what does she wish she'd known when she was first launching OneFile? "I wish I'd known how crucial it is to get out there and network. I don't think I met anyone other than potential customers in the first two years of trading. It was only when I started going to networking events and attending training courses that I realised the people around me could be of help. Their cumulative experience, advice and objective points of view were hugely valuable."

Typical of most entrepreneurs, Susanna's days are challenging and varied, though she relishes the control that comes from being the boss. "Our two young children wake me around 6am; once I've got us all ready, I take them to breakfast club at their school, arriving in the office around 8.00am. The commute on the tram gives me time to catch up with social media. During working hours, I'm either with the sales team, in strategic meetings with our partners or talking to customers. I often attend conferences and exhibitions, and more recently, I've been asked to speak at such events, which is a real honour. I can be away for a few days at a time, but I try and catch up with family or friends who live in the area I'm visiting."

Do the never-ending demands of business ever grate? "Some days are better than others," she admits. "I find it helpful to share my worries and frustrations with people in my network, who do the same with me. It's a relief and a comfort to know others understand what you're going through."

Officially, Susanna is a business owner. But more than that, she is every inch a successful entrepreneur. From spotting the gap in the market to developing the perfect solution and building OneFile to the industry giant it is today, she is undoubtedly an exemplary success. Incredibly grounded, and aware that entrepreneurs secretly thrive on learning new things, Susanna believes life would be dull if she knew everything there is to know.

High:

"Winning the Queen's Award for Innovation was a fantastic achievement for the whole team – it's one of the highest accolades there is in business. On a personal level, winning FL National Awards & Summit's 'Overall Businesswoman of the Year' was a heart-stopping moment. I remember sitting at the awards, listening to the host describing the achievements and personal qualities of the winner. I turned to my mum and said, 'She sounds amazing! What a woman!' After a moment, she leant over and whispered, 'they're talking about you!'"

Low:

Everything appeared to be going well until a mix-up meant their first member of staff wasn't paid. Susanna recalls, "She left soon after. She probably thought we didn't have any money and we were about to go bust! Obviously, we would all like to make the right decision the first time, but if we do not make mistakes how can we ever hope to learn?"

Golden Nugget:

"This probably won't be ground-breaking to read, but my biggest tip is this: remember that people buy from the people they like. I had no idea if I was a good salesperson or not until I went to my first sales training event. It boosted my confidence no end to realise I was doing everything I should – all I'd really done was be myself."

Advice to others:

"Get a mentor – preferably one already working in the type of business you'd love to emulate. Having a sounding board for ideas is invaluable; you can't hope to know everything if it's something you've not done before."

11
TURNING YOUR PASSION FOR WELLBEING INTO A MULTIMILLION BUSINESS

Small steps make a big difference

Nicola Elliott – Neom Organics

Nicola Elliott was so passionate about the positive effects of natural oils she decided to change her career and launch a business around them.

She says, "I was working as a journalist and had an incredibly busy lifestyle. I often burned the candle at both ends, and my wellbeing suffered as a result. My sleep was poor, I had no energy, my moods were up and down, and I began to feel anxious. It was clear I'd not been looking after myself and that things had to change. It was natural, due to my training, to research potential answers and solutions. I became interested in nutrition and what I was putting into my body, as well as aromatherapy and similar methods to make myself feel better. Once I changed my diet and explored natural products further, I saw my moods and energy levels lift, and I also began to sleep better."

As Nicola shared her experience with her friends, she found that no matter what their age or lifestyle, almost all of them were suffering from one or more of the same symptoms she had experienced. "Their issues and discomfort seemed to be dismissed as simply the fallout of modern times. I knew this wasn't the case, and I felt passionately that I could help people."

Nicola subsequently retrained as a nutritionist and aromatherapist. She left journalism to launch Neom Organics with her business partner, Oliver. They cobbled together their savings, and she also sold her car in order to create their own complex, targeted blends using 100% natural oils.

As a skilled storyteller, it was easy for Nicola to bring the brand to life. Her passion helped to make Neom Organics' products amazing, and the duo were very clear about their message. Nicola admits she's always working on the oils. "I'm tough on our products and meticulously test everything. I ask myself: is it the best it can be? Does it really work brilliantly?"

Customers clearly liked what they bought and returned for more. It also helped that the brand received an early endorsement from Kylie Minogue. "Kylie turned to natural products when recovering from cancer and said she often burned our 'Feel Refreshed' candles before she went on stage. That's no surprise, really – they're fabulous for giving users a boost of natural energy."

However, the company's growth wasn't an overnight success, even if Kylie did love their candles. Nicola recognised early on that the business had the potential for scale, but she says building such growth was done brick by brick. "There was no one thing that contributed to the company's success. Word of mouth and the strength of the brand grew with every new listing in a beautiful spa, every new product and every new shop we opened. The latter is always amazing; people really get to know the story behind the brand and come for treatments. They also take our test to see what their own wellbeing needs are. All we aim to do is tell people what we are about and how we can help them."

The products sound fantastic, but are they all that's needed for a successful business? "People are important, too," adds Nicola. "Our people have the power to make or break the business. We do everything we can to keep our brilliant team engaged and inspired. We've just moved into a gorgeous new office and offer free Pilates sessions each week. We also hold wellbeing festivals, encourage book clubs, dog walking, feel-good gatherings and parties – it's the little things that make a big difference."

The company uses various technological solutions and systems to help things run smoothly. "That said, we're in the process of getting them to talk to each other," Nicola laughs. "Aside from external systems, nothing beats face to face – in other words, simply talking to people. I get teased for liking notepads and paper diaries, but it's just that my brain works better if I can jot things down. I draw everything – all my ideas come to me in picture form."

Has entrepreneurship come as naturally as the passion for her products? "It's way harder than I thought it would be! The line between work and hobby has become blurred because I love what I do so much. I don't always want to switch off. I enjoy blogging and chatting on Instagram, and I test products in the bath with my little girl … it doesn't seem like work.

"Success at the outset would have been Neom being the biggest and best brand in the industry – and I think we are there. Oliver and I still have lots of plans for the company – we're both ambitious. Now that we know how much people love our products from the chats we have with them online and in person, we want to spread our story and message even further. I think success now is about enjoying everything we've achieved."

Unsurprisingly, Nicola's core motto is "small steps make a big difference". "It's plastered all over our office, on the walls in our stores, on our packaging and within our blogs. It's my key belief. Take the little moments and make them work for you. You could sit in the office toilets and create your own oasis of calm. It doesn't have to be 'yoga on the beach'. I personally make sure I eat good, nutritious food. I take a long bath every night, without fail, and ensure I get eight hours' sleep. Exercise helps, and I use our 'Scent to De-stress' several times during the day. I also make time to see my family and friends, and take 10 minutes a day to meditate. If all else fails, I unplug altogether."

Nicola's day starts with a cup of tea in bed with her kids. "We chat about the day, though they probably spend most of that time fighting over who has more toast! I try and keep my cool as I put a million bags – which should have been packed the night before, but weren't – into the car. After I've dropped the kids off and can hear myself think, I make calls in the car on the way to work. Most mornings involve a meeting with the marketing director and creative team, where we discuss product development and promotional campaigns.

"My diary constantly changes, and I always seem to have too many meetings. Towards the end of the day, my husband picks the kids up. Most nights I'm home to make tea, though, as I like cooking."

Nicola has gone from writing about the news to being in it – with fantastic achievements under her belt, better health and a richer quality of life in the process. You'd be hard-pressed to find a better definition of success.

High:

"Opening our first shop in Wimbledon was as significant as giving birth to my kids. I'll never forget it."

Low:

"I've learned how to not sweat the small stuff. I did far too much of that in the beginning, but it taught me to keep focused on the bigger picture … to ask myself, 'Will this issue still be as significant three years down the line?'"

Golden nugget:

"Be original. Don't copy anyone, as someone will find out or your customers will see through it."

Advice for others:

"A well-known name once told me it would take nine years to become a household brand. I think they were right. That's why you've got to have fun, as it's a long road – if you don't enjoy it, you've lost already. The journey really is as important as the destination."

12
TURNING YOUR CREATIVITY INTO AN ETHICAL JEWELLERY BUSINESS

Trust your own instincts

Harriet Kelsall – Harriet Kelsall Bespoke Jewellery

Harriet is another woman who never set out to be an entrepreneur or business owner, despite creating her first product – a ring – when she was just four years old. Yet, during her 20 years in business, she has been a trailblazer within her industry, ultimately establishing a new commercial model that others would go on to adopt.

Harriet Kelsall Bespoke Jewellery creates one-off, affordable pieces that reflect the personality and experiences of the people commissioning them. Made to a wonderfully high quality, each piece is intended to suit the individual's style and become something they wear all the time for the rest of their life.

Commissioning your own jewellery may be a normal occurrence now, but it hasn't always been that way. Says Harriet, "Twenty years ago, people didn't have beautiful jewellery made for them unless they had bucketloads of money and directions to Bond Street. Or, they may have known a bloke with tools, ably equipped to make something, but whose work would most likely lack any hint of uniqueness or design. Yet from an early age, I designed one-off pieces – though my dad was a GP, he was also a talented jeweller who taught me everything he knew."

While she was at university, Harriet studied industrial design, which she says gave her further insight into creating products. She then took a full-time job as an engineering manager while designing and making commissions for friends, and friends of friends, in her spare time. After work, she would come home and spend hours working on her jewellery in her garden shed, which she converted into a makeshift studio.

One evening, she looked at her waiting list and realised she knew none of the 30 customers' names on there. It occurred to her then that there was demand for her creations beyond just her immediate circle. Although she didn't recognise it at the time, she'd essentially been researching her market and trying out her business during the many evenings she spent making pieces for friends in her shed.

She says, "It was a while before I took the plunge and launched the business properly. I wasn't sure I had the confidence to do it professionally. What I was doing was so different to that of other jewellery designers who created entire ranges they then tried to sell to retailers. Yet I couldn't see why everyone had to have the same thing. I knew commissions didn't have to cost the earth, but because no one else was taking my approach, I almost convinced myself that there had to be a reason for this.

"I forged on anyway. It took me some years to realise that 'reachable bespoke design' hadn't existed on the high street because no one else had had the nerve to do it. It was down to me that it came to market, then everyone else followed."

Harriet proved she was an innovator when she uploaded details of her fledgling business onto a new-fangled invention: the internet. "This was at a time when even Google didn't exist. The worldwide web had just landed, and few people knew about it. I had a very basic website (just a landing page with my details and a picture of my work); it proved an effective route to market for me before the idea had even crossed my competitors' minds.

"Around the same time, a lady in Scotland needed an emergency tiara for her wedding. The shop she'd ordered the original piece from had let her down at the last minute. She called me on the Thursday as she was getting married on the Saturday. Back then, you couldn't email pictures over – snail mail was the norm for that sort of thing – but we didn't have time for that. I asked her if she'd heard of the internet, and she said she thought her brother's friend used it in his job. I told her to go to his house, and I sketched some ideas, uploaded them to my website and gave her the web address. Within a few hours, she'd chosen her design, which I made immediately, and which I also managed to post to her in time for the wedding.

She was absolutely thrilled! That's when I realised how handy this internet thing was, and how it might catch on!

"We redesigned the website when technology advanced, though I quickly realised that it's not simply a matter of having a beautiful digital shopfront. Having a website is a bit like opening a shop; if you open it on a country lane in the middle of nowhere, no one will ever find it. You have to drive people to it, which is the equivalent of picking it up and moving it to a busy high street. We do this via SEO and social media, particularly Instagram."

Harriet has learned a lot about marketing during her years as an entrepreneur – so much so that she's written a book about starting and marketing a creative business: *The Creative's Guide To Starting A Business: How To Turn Your Talent Into A Career*. She says, "Effective marketing means understanding your customers – who they are, and why what you offer will appeal to them. Then you need to talk to them in a way they will understand and connect with."

Joining the industry's trade association also proved a good move for Harriet, and she was eventually asked to sit on, and then chair its national committee. "It helped to raise my profile and boosted my reputation. It also meant journalists paid attention to what I was doing."

Ethics have always played a huge part in Harriet's business model. Hers was the first independent jeweller in the world to be certified by the Responsible Jewellery Council and be licensed by the Fairtrade Foundation. "When I first started the business, few people were interested in our ethics. Nowadays, though, customers really care about the people at the bottom of the supply chain. What we used to do out of altruism is now something we can shout about, and it's a real asset. I am often asked to talk nationally and internationally about Fairtrade gold, and how companies can be more responsible with regards to their suppliers. Whenever I do a talk like this, we gain customers from that audience – it's a form of marketing that we never expected."

So, how did the business grow from its initial beginnings in the garden shed? "I launched the brand with £400 I had left from the sale of my flat (I'd just bought a house with my boyfriend at the time). This paid for leaflets – which proved a waste of money in hindsight – web hosting, heating and lighting, and materials. My spare room became the workshop, and I saw customers at my kitchen table in those early days.

"After a year, I was able to move into a unit on a farm – this was momentous at the time. It felt good to separate my home and work space; although I love what I do, I can sometimes struggle to put work down. Not long after that, I was able to take on my first employee, Deborah, who's still with me today. I remember working out that I could just about afford her wages for four months (which amounted to more than I was taking home!). She soon earned her keep, though, and this allowed me to do more consultations and make more jewellery."

Sales continued to grow, and Harriet took the first step towards scaling the business by employing someone to make the jewellery for her. "Richard made the decision easy as he was a brilliant maker – much better at goldsmithing than I was."

Next came the company's first bricks-and-mortar shop. "I'd noticed that people were interested in seeing my other work when coming to discuss a commission. They'd buy necklaces or rings in addition to their original order. It also helped to give them design ideas."

A second shop in central Cambridge followed in 2005. Harriet remembers it as a "scary, expensive risk": "This was a huge learning curve for us. We realised that we had to be true to who we were, and not attempt to be 'high street' just because we *were* on a high street. By sticking to our values, we offered a unique experience. We had no sales people, only qualified designers who shared their knowledge with customers. They received the same service whether they were purchasing a ready-made necklace or commissioning a bespoke engagement ring."

It certainly sounds like it's been a straightforward, lucrative journey; demand has consistently outstripped supply, and all growth has been sustained. Does the business have any pressure points? Says Harriet, "We're still a small team, so holidays and sickness have to be carefully managed. I admit I found it difficult the first time a staff member went on maternity leave. However, I found that team members are often even better when they return to work as new mums. They're masters at prioritising, multitasking and organising things – such skills are well worth the expense of their leave. My team is 80% female; this isn't by design, we've always just employed the best person for the job.

"Scaling the business was only possible because I made the conscious decision to employ other talented designers, and not keep all the creativity to myself. The risk is that they could become competition, but if they're in their dream job, receiving a good wage, and they enjoy working for you, why would they leave?"

In 2018, the company reached another milestone with the opening of their studio and shop in Primrose Hill. Expanding into London represented a huge achievement for Harriet and her team, which includes 16 designers within a workforce of 34.

Given that Harriet never intended to have her own business, is it everything she thought it would be? "I am first and foremost a jewellery designer, who simply wanted everyone to be able to own and enjoy beautiful, individual pieces. I don't think I even knew what an entrepreneur was when I first started out though, looking back, I can see that I am one. I believe it's a term for someone innovative who brings new ideas to market.

"I feel that being dyslexic has been a huge advantage. Dyslexic minds think in layers, like onions, so we think about the problems around problems. When you are running a business, a lot of your time is spent sorting issues out. It used to annoy me, and I just saw problems as things that got in the way of my real work. One day it dawned on me that problem-solving *was* my main job – as the founder and as an entrepreneur."

The vision for Harriet when launching the business was to have a workshop and four or five people working for her. When that was realised, her aim was then to grow into a larger workshop and acquire a shop. Now that she's seen this happen, what's next on the horizon? "The vision keeps morphing! Though my future plans are very much connected to the business, they also involve helping our young people flourish and grow. I love training and supporting the next generation so that they can become brilliant jewellers."

Harriet Kelsall describes a day in her life as "changeable". She visits the company's shops at least once a week and continues to engage her team while working on all areas of the business. Her voluntary commitments – such as her position as non-executive director with the National Association of Jewellers, among others – also keep her busy. She doesn't ever think of herself as stressed, as she believes this insinuates that something is beyond her control: "I think people who talk about being stressed just mean they're very busy. It's within your control to do that work, solve that problem, tackle that issue. That's not to say you have to do everything yourself; the solution could be as simple as hiring the relative expert to sort things out."

Harriet is a strong advocate of networking in business. She says, "Sharing tips really helps. It's okay to work long hours and take your work home with you, as long as you enjoy it. Society often encourages us to resent working hard, and there are numerous experts out there charging good money to help people achieve a good work/life balance. To me, when you're a creative, your art isn't something you do for money – you just have to do it. You're driven to create."

High:

A high point for me would be being a key part of the team who launched Fairtrade Gold in 2011 or possibly becoming the chair of the National Association of Jewellers in 2018. It is important to mention opening the shop in London in 2018 somewhere in the text, but I would definitely not say that this was my business highlight to date.

Low:

I would say that my lowest point was the time when I had to cope with a lot of personal stuff – 8 miscarriages and then open heart surgery between 2009-2012, as it became really hard to keep totally focussed on the business whilst also dealing with poor health. My brilliant team helped me get through it though and I was soon back driving the business again.

Golden nugget:

"Art isn't something you do for money – you just have to do it. You're driven to create."

Advice for others:

"One of my traits which I've also observed with other female entrepreneurs is the tendency to see all aspects of one's life linked up rather than compartmentalised as 'work', 'personal', 'family' or 'friends'. This means that I work best when I am happily combining these things daily. When you are creative your creativity is part of who you are all of the time and in order to flourish creatively you need to feel OK about other aspects of your life too. I have noticed that a lot of men tend to compartmentalise and as many women have learned to mimic this masculine style of business. I think this can sometimes be harmful to a female in business.

"Never trust the business consultants. You may think that because they're experts in their field, they will know more than you do about your business. They really don't, and they definitely don't know how to grow your business better than you – or where to prioritise the investment of your hard-earned money. Trust your own instincts."

13
TURNING YOUR PASSION FOR DANCING INTO A GLOBAL FRANCHISE

Live life to the full and reach for the stars

Claire O'Connor – babyballet®

Though many businesses are built to be scalable and have big ambitions from the outset, this wasn't necessarily the case for babyballet®, despite its current spread across four countries and its sale of more than 100 franchise licences.

Claire Connor began the business because of her own childhood experience of dancing. She says, "I loved all types of dance, but when I went to dance school, I felt I was the wrong shape and size. I knew I wasn't the best, but unfortunately, only the best seemed to be accepted; there wasn't much emphasis on dancing just because you enjoyed it. I left at 14 with a lack of confidence, a poor body image and a dent in my self-esteem."

When Claire became a mum, she suffered from post-natal depression, and also faced the challenges that came with being a single parent. "I helped my mother run her dance school as it was difficult to find a job that suited my circumstances." It was then that Claire realised not much had changed. She noticed that the negativity she'd experienced hadn't gone away.

"I saw so few children who felt proud of who they were, and I wanted to change things. I wanted them to feel confident as they left dance classes, and excited about their potential – however advanced that was. I didn't want them to waste their time comparing themselves to others as I had done. Dance isn't just about ability; it teaches key social and physical skills. The environment needed to be more caring and supportive, not competitive and cut-throat."

Claire carried out some research and decided to create ballet classes for babies, toddlers and young children. She launched babyballet® in her home town of Halifax, West Yorkshire, UK in 2005. "The demand for classes was astounding – I couldn't put them on fast enough!" she recalls. "Children and their parents loved the ethos and the experience of the classes. I created a magical world of dance, filled with characters, colour, music – and above all, fun! A world where every child felt valued. I wanted as many children as possible to enjoy what we provided, which gave me the confidence to expand."

Her research showed that there was no other pre-school ballet franchise in existence. "That was when I thought, 'It has to be me!' I invested a huge amount of time, blood, sweat and tears into the creation of a franchise model. It had to be successful for the franchisees, and it also had to maintain the exceptional standards of the babyballet® syllabus and brand."

Claire remortgaged her house, sold her car, borrowed money from family and took out a bank loan to finance the expansion. She never wavered in her faith that it would be a success. "When I sold the first franchise, I felt a true sense of achievement. Someone else could see the potential and believed in what I'd worked so hard to develop. As more franchisees came on board, I loved seeing these women and men, these mums and dads, running their own successful businesses."

Claire didn't stop there. Merchandise and uniform ranges were designed and made; parties, events and shows were held; and characters, created – all of which gave the business further income streams. Recruiting staff to help manage the business soon became necessary. Claire cites her recruiting of staff as instrumental to ensuring the business reached the next level: "I'd become maxed out on my own. I was so fortunate to have found people with the same passion, ethos and commitment as me. The business wouldn't be where it is today without their input."

The marketing of babyballet® was a mix of word of mouth and digital. An appearance on the programme 'Big Ballet' also raised Claire's profile. She recalls, "I was reluctant to audition, but it turned out to be a great opportunity. The documentary was close to my heart, as it challenged the issues of body shape. I was able to put my demons to rest and achieve a lifelong dream – appearing in a real ballet."

Claire didn't set out to be an entrepreneur, even though she clearly embodies the word. "It really did just happen," she says. A wonderful milestone was the business's tenth anniversary. "I never believed I could grow a business, as someone who lacked confidence. The idea was sound, but my lack of ability and business experience almost held me back. When we passed the fifteen-year point with 100 franchisees and licensees, I took the time to reflect on everything we'd achieved. I'm someone who's usually quick to self-criticise, but I actually felt proud of myself for a change."

A CRM and online booking system helps Claire and her team, and also the franchisees, to be more efficient. In the beginning, Claire felt as if she had to 'do it all', but she now realises how much more effective she is when she is concentrating on her core strengths. "I wish I'd believed in what I'm naturally good at a lot sooner and delegated more."

A typical day for Claire, as a self-confessed 'morning person', means an early start. Between getting herself ready for the day ahead, Claire has the children and the dog to sort out. She says she's better with self-discipline nowadays and much more efficient. "I can't say I'm cured, but I'm trying," she admits.

In between school hours, Claire works on the business: supporting the team, visiting potential franchisees, attending business events and developing new ideas. She dedicates one day a week to ironing out issues with her finance and operations director, where they swap ideas on business development and discuss key decisions.

Later, things like childrens' clubs, making the tea, sorting uniform and checking school bags take precedence – typical 'mum' jobs that have to be done, however successful one is: "I chill out too. I'm not a big TV fan, so winding down for me may mean going to the gym, playing a game with the family or reading."

Success comes at a price, so the saying goes, and Claire's journey has been no easier than anyone else's. "I didn't use to manage stress well," she confesses. "The first ten years were pretty manic, and I'd become so accustomed to feeling like that – to everything being 100 miles an hour – that I had actually forgotten what it felt like without stress. I think I'd been on the roller-coaster for so long, I didn't know how to get off it. Once I recognised this, though, I worked hard to change my mindset.

"Exercise always makes me feel better, and I try to go to the gym at least three times a week – more if I'm able. It always does me good; even if I'm not physically in the office, I think about work a lot. Exercise helps me to switch off."

High:

"Seeing children enjoying the programme, and knowing more and more are able to access our classes, makes me so happy. We'll get social media posts from children anywhere in the world, saying how much fun they're having – it's an absolute joy to hear that. I also take great pleasure in knowing my franchisees are making money, achieving great things and having a taste of success with their own business – one that fits around their family/lifestyle. I couldn't ask for more than that."

Low:

"I've spent too much time beating myself up about the things I'm not good at, which is why it's so important to me to instil confidence in the next generation."

Golden nugget:

"Spend 15 minutes every evening planning everything for the next day, whether that's home, family, or both. That way, there's no mad panic in the morning, because once you start the day stressed, you are likely to spend the rest of it trying to catch up, and never feeling quite in control."

Advice to others:

"Be kind to yourself. There's always something you could be working on when it comes to your business, so make sure you take satisfaction and feel pleased about the things you have achieved in a day, and not focus on the things you still have to do. Technology is there to serve us. Don't be a slave to the 'ping' of your phone."

14
BUILDING THE DIGITAL MARKETING AGENCY OF THE FUTURE

Never say never

Lauren Stevenson – Aisle 8

Securing clients such as Ferrari mere months after launch, and then turning over a million pounds in the second year of the business, means Lauren Stevenson is no stranger to success. As someone who engaged marketing companies and PR agencies as part of her in-house role in retail, the idea for Aisle 8 – which she runs with her business partner, Virginia Morris – stemmed from understanding exactly what a customer wants and needs from such services.

Back then, Lauren could see that the digital landscape was changing, and that it was starting to dominate advertising and PR. It didn't seem as if the agencies Lauren worked with had fully grasped this, as instead they relied on print media and similar traditional methods to shout about clients' brands. Lauren could see there was space in the market for a company unafraid to do things differently, a company that would fully embrace and employ new technologies.

Together with Virginia, she launched Aisle 8 – an agency that delivers digitally remastered communications and acts as an extension to its clients' teams. "We believed in our idea and plan for the business, and we launched Aisle 8 with our savings, never once thinking things wouldn't work out. Luckily, others also recognised the potential of the internet and how it was shaping every industry, and we were able to negotiate a £30k overdraft quite early on."

By focusing on specific industries, Lauren felt they could make their brand a strong one. "Being all things to all people dilutes your resources and attention. We wanted to build the business slowly, working with the right brands and putting the right teams in place. The three divisions we focus on are lifestyle, fashion and beauty. We must be doing something right, given that our clients continue to work with us rather than the many competitors we have in this industry. I believe we have created an infectious culture that others want to be part of."

Word about the company did indeed travel, and today it is very successful, with a team of 26 working behind the scenes. "Systems such as stockroom management technology, contact databases and financial software streamline operations help the team to do their jobs. As you'd expect, social media has had a huge impact on our business, not just for our clients, but also when we promote Aisle 8."

That's not to say the business doesn't encounter any challenges – cash flow being one. Lauren says, "As with most businesses, we've got to keep our eye on the funds coming in and going out. We have to pay our suppliers before we charge our clients, which carries a certain degree of risk. It's not something we can ever forget about. PR is another aspect that can go one way or the other. You can't guarantee coverage, and you're at the mercy of an editor's keyboard. It's not something we can control every aspect of, which can be difficult to explain to clients."

Lauren values her partnership with Virginia; she knows that, for her at least, two heads are better than one. She adds, "I love being an entrepreneur and running a business, but I don't think anyone can ever be prepared for what's ahead of them when they start out – if I'd have known, I may not have done it! Don't get me wrong – the highs are fantastic, but the lows are exactly how they sound, and the emotional pressure is tough. I count myself lucky that I have a supportive business partner who allows me to offload whenever I need to.

"The business has always felt like a success, in that I was in control of my destiny from day one, and it was clear our idea had legs. I feel blessed that I can be anywhere in the world at any given time, and that I get up every morning to do a job I absolutely love."

Lauren cites a good workout as key to managing the stresses and strains that come with running a successful business. She pounds the treadmill at Barry's Bootcamp every morning before heading to the office, using the commute as an opportunity to deal with her inbox. Once there, she drinks copious amounts of coffee and has her daily pep talk with Virginia before catching up with the team. Her days vary – they can be spent with clients or at media meetings, pitching ideas and writing strategy, or can be all hands on deck prepping for an event.

It's clear clients of Aisle 8 like the way the duo do things, and find the company's approach refreshing. Brands as big as Ferrari wouldn't move their communications to the new kids on the block if they didn't see value in their offering; winning the supercar manufacturer's contract six months after launching Aisle 8 was a huge acknowledgement they were on the right path.

Lauren sums up her journey: "I couldn't have dreamt things would turn out the way they have, but once I saw what we could bring to the market, it was more difficult to turn away and forget about it than it was to take the idea and run with it. If anyone reading this is thinking of starting their own business, don't wait for the perfect time, because it will never happen. Do it now!"

High:

"The day we moved into our offices. We'd designed them and had them built from scratch to fit our requirements. That was a real 'pinch me' moment for the whole team."

Low:

"Initially, we said yes to brands that weren't the best fit for Aisle 8. We've learnt from this, and nowadays choose clients that are as right for us as we are for them."

Golden nugget:

"Don't try to run before you can walk, however tempting it may be. It's easy to get carried away and to want everything 'now'. Most successful businesses are built carefully and steadily; they're more robust and resilient that way."

Advice to others:

"The belief in what you're doing can get you most of the way to where you need to be, but remember, you're only human. Some of my greatest successes have been as a result of mistakes I've made. Never say never. I remember once saying that I'd never want to have my own business. At that point in time, I couldn't think of anything worse. Look where I am now!"

15
BUILDING A BUSINESS AROUND SOLVING QUALITY ISSUES

You can't be all things to all people

Kate Krachai – Quality Context

Being passionate about your business idea is a must, particularly when difficult decisions need to be made and constant challenges threaten your enthusiasm. Kate Krachai was certainly passionate about her business idea – a quality (pardon the pun) her competitors lacked.

During her early career in industry, Kate noticed quality was something of an inconvenience to companies. She says, "It was seen as a distraction or a blocker, whereas I saw it as an enabler. Colleagues told me that I'd be good at bringing quality to life, so I launched Quality Context with a view to understanding clients in a way others were failing to do; I wanted to get under the skin of customers' businesses and make quality exciting."

Quality Context works with pharmaceutical companies and healthcare organisations to uphold patient safety and ensure high-quality medicines are consistently delivered. Their mission is to enhance quality, reduce risk and improve regulatory compliance. In addition to helping clients navigate legislation, their services also include analytical testing, consultancy support, importation and secondary packaging solutions. Says Kate, "Many well-known products and medicines for day-to-day use have passed through our laboratory for testing."

The company started small, using their cash flow to fund everything. Networking proved to be the best way forward for Kate: "We've always been well connected, and the company continually receives fantastic feedback. We do great work and our clients pass on their experience to people they know. It's proved the best marketing strategy for us, having others spread the word."

Growth continued to be self-supported at almost every stage; however, more recently, the company secured growth fund money and received investment from their bank, which they used to purchase necessary equipment. Says Kate, "Borrowing was a scary concept at first, but I've learned that you have to invest in a business for it to grow."

And grow it certainly has. Kate has steered Quality Context through a number of milestones that have all contributed to the company's expansion. She recalls some of the most significant milestones: "Taking on my first employee was scary and a huge leap. Then, when I hired our first technical manager, I could really see that the business was scalable as I was no longer doing all the billable work. The business was starting to exist beyond me, which was fabulous and very exciting!

"The next tipping point was in 2013, when we opened our own laboratory. This changed our status as a company; we were no longer an agency but a tangible business with long-term plans.

"Within just a few years, we'd outgrown those premises, and subsequently moved into much larger facilities. This was further proof that we'd firmly established our identity within the industry."

She cites cash flow as the most stressful element within the business, although software such as XERO and Harvest helps Kate and her team keep on top of it. "I'm lucky my fellow director predominantly handles this area and shoulders some of the burden. There are other responsibilities that can also weigh heavily – such as ensuring we meet clients' requirements and their deadlines.

"Knowing when to hire can also affect the internal balance; hiring too soon can have a financial impact, but if you leave it too late, the team can feel overworked and under pressure. I'm always open about the stresses and strains both I and the company are under – not only does this help to engage the team towards our end goals, it also helps them to understand why I may have a short fuse some days!

"Being an entrepreneur is sometimes difficult. I didn't set out to conquer the business world, and it's a big responsibility knowing that all the decisions and the careers of your team rest on your shoulders – it's true what they say about the highs being high and the lows being low. All that said, it's a hugely enjoyable journey, and I'm glad I took it."

When she first launched Quality Context, Kate felt success was related to being paid and securing repeat custom. She says the hiring of others was another sign that she'd 'made it'. Nowadays, Kate measures success by how the company's growth is sustained, and the happiness of her team.

She has carved out a routine that works for her and the business. Three days a week Kate works school hours, so that she can take her daughter to school and be there to pick her up. On those days, she often reads emails in the evenings to offset the school run time and to keep on top of everything.

Balance is key to Kate, and it sounds like she's achieved that. Does she ever feel under stress? "Sometimes," she admits. "I have a few strategies that help, such as building in a little downtime and breathing space between meetings. I work at setting boundaries in and out of the office, and I also try to keep things in perspective. I do Pilates in my spare time, too, which helps me to wind down and think of other things."

With such an emphasis on quality, it's clear to see that Kate applies this to her time – both in work and at home – to ensure she gets the most out of every moment.

High:

"Winning awards is a real honour. Being recognised for corporate social responsibility (CSR) in our city region was hugely fulfilling. Others thinking you're worthy of mention is incredibly flattering."

Low:

In October 2018, I took the decision to close Quality Context. This is not a decision that I took lightly but one which we needed to take. The story of any business failure is defined by big decisions, small decisions and bad luck. Our story is no different. It was a combination of internal and external factors that pulled us down. In case you were wondering; yes, Brexit mattered. The only reason we survived so long after a torrid 2017 was because of the exceptional and caring team that surrounded me until the final day. I am sorry I wasn't able to get us to new pastures before we ran out of time.

Golden nugget:

"Surround yourself with excellent people – you can't do it alone. You need the support of others that have bought into your vision and who are as keen to go with you on your journey as you are."

Advice for others:

"You can't be all things to all people. Know your limitations and respect your own needs."

"Never employ someone you already know. You won't act the same with each other and it won't end well."

16
CARING FOR OTHERS MAKES EXCELLENT BUSINESS

Always treat others in the same way you yourself would like to be treated

Leanne Silverwood – Local Care Force

People-centred businesses tend to be more difficult to manage than product-centric enterprises, simply because so much is out of the owner's control. Though Leanne Silverwood of Local Care Force would agree with this statement, she is proof that using the right approach and investing in your people are two things that can make all the difference.

Leanne founded Local Care Force 13 years ago. The company supplies trained, experienced staff for the nursing, health and social care sectors. Their engaged, friendly team manage the logistics and compliance of placements, and their specialist trainers ensure every worker is fully equipped, both physically and mentally, to deliver care of the highest possible standard to all patients.

Leanne's own experience with care agencies was the driver behind her idea. Back then, she worked within in-patient mental health services, often alongside agency personnel. She witnessed at first-hand how ill-equipped and poorly trained most agency staff seemed to be, which had a massive impact on the level of care they were able to provide: "I noticed that they were wrongly placed, so they couldn't make the best use of their skill set; they didn't have the specialist knowledge they needed to be able to care for their patients properly in view of the various illnesses these people had; or, their personality wasn't suited to the job – empathy, patience and commitment were often lacking. I felt an agency that invested and focused on its staff would make a real difference to the people they cared for, as well as to the industry itself."

Hiring the right people was clearly a requisite for Leanne's business. "Having worked with agency staff, I knew the qualities I'd need to source. I also understood their role, the pressures they would be under, the type of clients they'd serve and the challenges they'd face. I therefore felt much better placed to source the right team than someone sitting in an office flicking through profiles on a computer."

Confident the quality of care her new company would provide spoke for itself, Leanne launched the business, putting a rigorous recruitment process in place. Her plan was long-term: after hiring and training the right people, she wanted to ensure they were placed in the correct positions. If she was going to uphold her company's quality of service, she also knew she had to trust, develop and appreciate her staff. As another huge commitment, considering the margins other care industry bosses claim are cripplingly tight, Leanne intended to pay her staff what they were worth.

Fast forward just a few months, and it soon became apparent Leanne's seemingly radical approach was just what the industry needed: "We put a lead clinical nurse in place to support the nurses and carers, and took great care to look after our office team's mental wellbeing, too. Having such a strong focus on our staff, as well as making the principles of clinical governance our cornerstone, we were inducted into The Royal College of Nursing's library of best practice. We were also shortlisted for some highly esteemed nursing awards, which had previously only been awarded to care providers and trusts. This all served to strengthen our voice and position in the industry."

For the first eight years of business, Leanne and her team didn't set aside any budgets for marketing, simply because they didn't need to. She says, "Word of mouth and a strong reputation have, by far, been the most effective means of marketing the business. More recently, we've recruited a social media and e-marketing expert to implement campaigns that will reach further than our current client base. I'm a firm believer in sticking to what I'm good at and letting other professionals do the same – being a jack-of-all-trades is not economically sustainable."

Leanne describes herself as having an "incredibly strong work ethic": "It's a trait I'm proud of. I'm naturally passionate (read: stubborn!), focused and driven. I roll up my sleeves and work hard to achieve success, both in my professional and personal relationships. I surround myself with people who share my vision and whom I trust implicitly."

Leanne thinks it's important to be a good role model when employing people: "Put in the hours and your team will, too. So many company owners take advantage of the luxury to do as they please. But if you're in late and leave early, it doesn't breed productivity. On the same note, don't be proud about what you do. Humility is key. I make coffee for visitors, fill the sweet bowl and fix running toilets – there's no place for a 'that isn't my job', or 'that's beneath me' attitude."

Local Care Force has had its fair share of challenging times, not least when the last recession hit. Sticking to its guns when everyone around them panicked, Leanne believes, helped the company grow even further: "There was never a question that we wouldn't be able to uphold our service levels. Other agencies were slashing their prices and opting for cheap online training while we continued to invest in our staff, using the same in-person, face-to-face, simulated training we'd always provided. Clients who left us for cost reasons came back within a few months, citing poorly trained staff, multiple incidents and their fears over safety as reasons to return."

Of course, being a people-centric business, it only takes one bad apple to upset the cart. Says Leanne, "One wrong person in our business can damage morale and our reputation in the short term, which is why it's so important that we recruit well. The happiness of my team is integral to the company's success.

"To help us succeed in this aim, we developed an app to encourage peer recognition. We saw that feedback on a daily basis mattered to our staff. Every person on the team identifies a colleague on the app and feeds back to them; they also proactively support them should an opportunity arise. This can be anything from covering their work while they visit a client, helping them through a relationship breakdown, baking them a cake or simply making them smile. The app then selects a 'monthly legend' who goes on to win prizes. I strongly believe in affirmation: each month everyone in the business receives an email full of genuine and positive (and anonymous) comments from their peers. We've seen a significant rise in the confidence of our team, and it's a joy to work in a kind, respectful workplace."

You can feel the pride Leanne has for her team through these words. She sounds like a great boss, but is she a typical entrepreneur? She laughs, "I only realised I was an entrepreneur when I won awards that said so! It's not a word I use as it sounds self-serving to me, but when I do look back at what I've achieved, I appreciate that I'm worthy of the title. So, yes, I am an entrepreneur. I've earned it and I'm proud!"

Leanne has herself received some fantastic recognition from her peers. She won *Yorkshire Post*'s Young Entrepreneur of the Year, then another award led to a 'Women of the Year' lunch with the Duchess of Cornwall. She was also named the top entrepreneur in Yorkshire by *Insider Business* magazine's '42 achievers under 42' list.

Leanne admits she wasn't the easiest person to manage when she was younger, and that being her own boss means everything. While her early goals were money-orientated, the outcome has changed. "It's not so much about the money I earn, but about having the funds to do what we do well. I employ the best trainers for the business and I pay my employees their worth; my team's happiness is so important to me. I also think success is being able to sleep at night knowing the people we support have appropriate care, as well as feeling assured that they're living their lives safely and with dignity."

It's no surprise that Leanne's favourite saying is "treat people how you want to be treated", given that this seems to be the story of her life and a virtue she exercises. She says, "I never cancel if I say I'm going somewhere/doing something. I always go above and beyond, so that people know they're important to me – from bringing a Zimbabwean colleague his favourite biltong from a market at King's Cross to sending a note to a friend to tell her how proud I am of her.

I naturally have a positive outlook, and I'm certainly a 'solutions' kind of person. It takes a lot to unbalance me – however, if I do feel stress, it's usually over little things, such as missing my train. I fear sleeping in and saying the wrong thing at the wrong time – 'foot in mouth syndrome' is a bit of an issue for me!"

Leanne may throw everything she has towards developing her team and satisfying her clients, however, she credits her own circle of support as fundamental to her success: "I have the most amazing team, family and friends, and I wouldn't be where I am today without them. I'm truly blessed."

High:

"When Local Care Force was listed as number 21 in *The Times*' Top 100. We also got the highest score (95%) out of all the companies listed.

"In a survey, 95% of my team said I was 'an inspiration to the workforce' – their respect meant everything. Of my team, 93% say that 'we live up to the company's values' (i.e., having fun at work) and 91% said they loved their role. We also came ninth among companies recognised for giving something back, which was a real highlight as we put so much time and effort into communities and our charity work. Overall, it was confirmation that we're doing something right."

Low:

"Some people turned out to be wolves in sheep's clothing. For a time, this had a negative impact on the team, and I felt I had let them down with my poor choices. The lesson I had to learn was that you can't let the morals of others affect your actions. Their behaviour speaks volumes about them, not you. You can only control what *you* do, and how *you* treat people."

Golden nugget:

"If you don't have any problems in your business, there's something very wrong. That said, you can choose what bothers you and what issue is not worth another moment's thought."

Advice for others:

"It's difficult to change the ethics and culture of your company, so start as you mean to go on. Stay positive and never exude stress – it's just as infectious as positivity. Have a gossip with your team, show them photos of your weekend outfit … engagement is real, it means something. A small break from work pressures improves productivity. I need these breaks, too, as I have a short attention span. If you manage your team well, your team will want to reflect that in their work."

17
CREATING A HEALTH CARE BUSINESS FROM SCRATCH

Making lemonade when you are handed lemons

Abigail Marshall – 1st Resource Recruitment

There are many different reasons why entrepreneurs choose such a life. Some crave the challenge; some launch businesses to solve specific problems; others simply want to be their own boss. It was the latter for Abigail Marshall, which ultimately led her to launch 1st Resource Recruitment. She needed time off for family care and hospital appointments, and a level of flexibility with regards to her working hours – both of which could have proved an issue had she remained employed.

She explains, "I had to give up my full-time management role after I had twins. My boys had a number of issues, and both were very ill; one was born with a narrow trachea while the other was being investigated for epilepsy. I literally lived in St. James's Hospital during the first few years of their lives. It was therefore crucial for me to find a way to earn money that meant I could work from home and set my own hours.

"I did some research and came across an advert online posted by a company seeking home-based recruiters. They provided all the training, admin and back-office support necessary in return for 40% of recruiters' profits. You could even choose the sector you wanted to work in. It was just what I looking for."

Abigail already had a good network of friends and contacts that worked within the health industry; although she knew how competitive a market it was, she felt she had the interest, passion and network to succeed. "I felt it was the ideal sector to work in. The world will always need doctors, carers and nurses," she says.

She duly joined the company and specialised in medical recruitment. The role allowed her to care for her children while earning a good income. Before long, however, Abigail was keen to strike out on her own. It was then that she launched 1st Resource. She spent £3k setting up the business, initially needing only a laptop and phone to run it. She also brought on board a partner, a nurse, who brought with her valuable technical knowledge.

Abigail continued to work for the home-based recruitment company until 1st Resource was more established. She says, "In that first year of business, my partner and I did everything ourselves, even some of the shifts!" After 12 months, however, Abigail left the other company to focus solely on developing her own business.

From her experience, Abigail knew that successful recruitment relies on good relationships, something she put into practice when she created 1st Resource: "It was absolutely crucial that we recruited the right calibre of staff for placements. I built a capable, reliable team of people who delivered everything we promised our clients without compromising our standards. The medical industry is conservative and quite traditional; they don't like the hard sell. If you do a good job and can be relied upon, they'll come back to you time and time again. We therefore didn't need to spend a lot of time and money marketing, although we did take advantage of any free advertising opportunities to recruit medical staff."

The company turned over £50k in its first year, something Abigail describes as "unimaginable". Clearly, it wasn't a fluke, as the company turned over £250k in its second year. "At that point, we'd employed more staff than I ever thought we could afford. I think the secret of our success was the way we treated our people, and how well we looked after our clients. We recognised that our employees were our greatest asset, and we offered them flexible hours and a good rate of pay. They were happy, our clients were happy, and it was their repeat business that saw us grow."

A recipe for success indeed. However, there are always challenges in business and Abigail has seen her fair share: "Cash flow is something we have to continually watch. Initially, the NHS offered 14-day payment terms, but this moved to 30, then 60, then 90 days before invoices were paid. As you can imagine, this causes an issue when you have people relying on you who can't wait that long for their wages.

"The first thing we did was consult our staff. They said they preferred a monthly wage, to be able to budget well; this helped us immensely. We also put a robust credit-management process in place and chased invoices every seven days. If things were particularly tight, we borrowed from friends and family rather than from the bank, which saved money in interest payments. With such initiatives in place, we were able to avoid invoice factoring."

Her life as a business owner isn't just about convenience; Abigail feels her experience with 1st Resource makes good use of her business degree: "I've always found it easy to translate theory into practice, and although I've faced some shocks along my entrepreneurial journey, these have helped shape my drive to succeed. I had a business mind even as a child, and I've enjoyed the process despite the odds. Initially, success was earning a living while being able to look after the children, but I've found it's just as important to me to make a difference, as well as to see my hard work translate into a decent financial return. And because I created the business to work around my family, I've never found it a problem to balance both areas of my life."

Launching, running and growing a business is a learning curve for anyone, and Abigail recognises that some elements come from personal experience rather than the classroom: "I wish I'd known that it was okay to chase clients over unpaid invoices; I initially felt uncomfortable reminding them their payment was due in case I lost their business. I've also learned how important it is to obtain a contract of sale with clients. It's much easier to refer back to the terms and conditions they initially agreed to if something goes wrong."

Her favourite saying is, "This too shall pass", which suggests she doesn't get bogged down by the finer details too often. "I make sure I exercise every day, and I also aim to go to bed as early as I can so that I get a good night's sleep. I volunteer my time to good causes, as I find this incredibly fulfilling. I coach the under-15 sprinters at Leeds City Athletic Club. I love coaching the girls and boys there – it's so rewarding.

"As a business owner, you never fully switch off or stop working; I just aim to do the best I can every day, and I find the next day takes care of itself. It's this act of taking one day at a time that helps me remain focused on the positives. I'm just someone who seeks solutions to problems rather than spending time weeping over them!"

High:

"Running the business is a high in itself. I enjoy the juggling of home and work life, earning a living and contributing to the community."

Low:

"When a client that owed us £66k went into administration, I still had to pay my staff for the work they'd done, knowing I'd never get that money back."

Golden nugget:

"The best advice I've ever been given is to never give up."

Advice for others:

"Everyone's journey is different, so don't feel tempted to compare. Stick to your own path, whatever the odds, and remain focused until you get to the finish line. If you come across an obstacle in your path, remember how far you've actually come – you already have the skills, tenacity and faith to overcome anything."

18
LEVERAGING YOUR SKILLS TO BUILD A RECRUITMENT BUSINESS

You have to embrace failure on your way to becoming a success

Stephanie Asplin – The Crewing Company Recruitment Ltd

Going from working in an industry to taking your skills and knowledge externally to fly solo may seem like a sound basis for a business, but it still takes a huge leap of faith – one that Stephanie Asplin took in 2006 when she set up her own specialist recruitment agency.

She began in children's television and was initially based in Manchester. There, she co-ordinated shows such as Ministry of Mayhem (MOM), hosted by Holly Willoughby.

After moving to London to work with the likes of Richard and Judy and Channel 4, she had what she calls her 'eureka' moment.

Part of Stephanie's role was to book various crews and programme editors. Although the status quo was adequate, she knew it could be so much better. She also felt there was an opportunity to deliver a first-class customer experience. That was the moment The Crewing Company – a multi-award-winning recruitment agency that specialised in the creative industries, incorporating a diverse selection of talent across broadcast, production (TV, film and corporate), advertising, PR, animation and new media – was born.

Stephanie sought the opinion of her family before making the actual jump. She says, "Most of my family gave me their full support, but my grandfather thought I was crazy to give up a steady job to launch a new business that had no security! He soon changed his mind when he saw it take off, though he was probably bored to tears when I discussed exit strategies with him on his 100th birthday!"

So, what was the key ingredient of The Crewing Company's success? "Doing something different. It wasn't just a case of being ahead of the competition; I knew I had to offer something unique. During my career it had been incredibly frustrating when booking all the staff needed for a project, as I had to contact three separate agencies. Each one only provided crew for their specific discipline: pre-production, crew or post-production. No one represented a one-stop shop or end-to-end solution. That was why I stood out. The Crewing Company covered all three sectors, making its clients' lives much easier."

Stephanie funded the launch by selling £5,000 of shares her father had left her in his will. She also worked weekends, organising regular pub quizzes. Getting the word out was the next part, via social media, word-of-mouth recommendations and exhibitions, among other things. She says, "About a year after launch, I heard about an industry exhibition called Broadcast Live. It seemed the type of event our potential clients would head to, but exhibiting there threatened to take all the funds I had. Nevertheless, I took the risk and bought a stand. While at the show I handed my business card to someone from a news agency. She called a few weeks later, asking for an editor for 20 days in Baghdad.

"I worked day and night to find someone suitably qualified who was available and willing to jump on a plane to go to a war zone. After a few 'tours of duty', our client stepped aside (she was actually a producer, not a recruiter), suggesting that we supplied the crew directly to her client. She even offered to write a letter of recommendation for us. It was the break we'd been looking for, which felt fantastic ... until a letter arrived. It read: 'We'd be absolutely delighted to write a letter of recommendation for £5,000.'

"We were still in the start-up stages, barely breaking even, and we struggled to justify the expense when there was no guarantee of any work. We decided to accept their offer, though I felt sick when their invoice cleared out our bank account. Despite this uncertainty, everything worked out well; that £5k risk brought in more than £5m worth of business, working on what has since become known as 'the most expensive media project the world has ever seen'."

That's an example of a strong gut instinct! But has every decision since then worked out as well? "There have been ups and downs, as you'd expect with any business. Our pressure point seems to be continual changes in legislation. In 2016, we could no longer work with self-employed freelancers, which cut our freelancing workforce by half. We now have a Head of Compliance, who is always 10 steps ahead of any changes in the law, so there are no surprises. Of course, staffing levels are crucial, as our people represent our biggest asset. Everything is built on relationships, and if a member of staff leaves us, it could mean that we lose a client, too."

To help the smooth day-to-day running of the company, The Crewing Company uses a system called Eclipse that holds information on clients, candidates and bookings. Stephanie is currently investing £80k into a new best-in-class recruitment Customer Relationship Management (CRM) system, which will integrate with the company's cloud-based back-office systems, as well as their online candidate portal. A mobile app will help freelancers manage their availability, submit timesheets and generate self-billing invoices. "Recruitment is about people, and good recruitment will always require human intervention," she adds. "While some people use tech to try and do away with the need for a recruitment consultant, we use it to better equip our consultants, so they can further develop their relationships with clients and candidates, i.e. to better understand and serve them. People are not digital."

Stephanie's parents passed on a strong work ethic. "To achieve in life, you have to graft!" she says, smiling as she recalls her parents' advice. Her father was a farmer and her mother was an entrepreneur who ran three private nursery schools in the UK and one in West Africa. By the age of 13, Stephanie had her own ironing business. Clearly, it seems, the apple doesn't fall far from the tree.

"I enjoy being an entrepreneur, but I hadn't accounted for the stress that comes with employing people. I feel a genuine disappointment when a member of staff says they're moving on. I have a wonderful management team I will never take for granted. My very first employee, CJ Dalton, is now our director of operations. My husband left his full-time job to work for the company; both are integral to the business. It wouldn't be where it is today without them.

"Success is happy clients, happy candidates and a happy team – and that's something that's never changed for me. The business may be at its most profitable, but if it's not a happy place for anyone to be, you can't class it as a success."

Stephanie's favourite saying is, "Always leave people better than you find them". Is there anything she regrets? "I learn something new every week, but one of my greatest lessons is not to make work my entire life. You have to switch off the emails every now and then. If your business consumes you, you can't look at things from different angles, or understand how to drive it forward."

Each morning starts with a two-hour commute. Stephanie spends the first couple of hours in the office catching up with developments and planning for meetings, then connects with her team and clients. There's no time for lunch ("I just eat at my desk!") and the late afternoon sees her attacking her to-do list, responding to the day's enquiries and emails, before finishing at 7pm and making the two-hour trip home.

With such a full-on-sounding schedule, how does she cope? "Plenty of wine!" she laughs. "Seriously though, I've had to work on this. In the early days, everything lands on your shoulders, and it can wear you down after a while. I've come to accept that there are never enough hours in the day to do everything. I simply focus on what needs to be done first."

High:

"Winning 'Best Freelancer Recruitment Team of the Year' at the Marketing and Digital Awards in 2016. I also won 'Recruitment Boss of the Year' at the same event. It was amazing to celebrate with my team, who deserved the accolades every bit as much as I did."

Low:

"Five years in, we were approached by a group of complementary businesses, who suggested we pooled our resources and created an end-to-end integrated-service provider. The cost to join the group was 10% equity of The Crewing Company, as well as steep management fees; in return, we'd receive business development and management support from the directors of the parent company. As the Iraqi deal was due to end, we took our next big risk and signed up.

"On paper, the vision for the group was fantastic, but as time went on, it became clear that executing might be a problem. We ended up spending more and more time on group problems than in our own business, and knew we had to cut our losses and get out. It cost us £40k to buy back our 10%. Hindsight is wonderful; however, I'm a firm believer that everything happens for a reason. It certainly made us stronger."

Golden nugget:

"Never assume anything. Write everything down. And never try to look bigger than you are; if you're a small, boutique company, be proud of this. Don't be afraid to highlight your strengths."

Advice for others:

"Risk is something you're bound to encounter as an entrepreneur. Take as many of the informed, calculated risks that you can, as this will grow your business. I've also learned to do my homework and research our market, as well as to learn from any mistakes. Always leave people better than you find them."

19
BUILDING A FINANCIAL WEALTH-MANAGEMENT BUSINESS

You never know what's around the corner – always grab life with both hands

Jillian Thomas – Future Life Wealth Management

A brush with death, although utterly terrifying, can ultimately have a positive impact on survivors' lives. It can also serve as a reminder that we never know what's around the corner – and that we should grab every opportunity life gives us with both hands.

This was certainly the case for Jillian Thomas, who launched Future Life Wealth Management after she was caught up in the 2004 Indian Ocean Boxing Day earthquake and tsunami. She describes the disaster as "the worst thing that's happened to me, but also the best". It forced her to take stock of her life, in more ways than one.

At the time, Jillian worked in financial planning as an independent financial adviser (IFA). Even though she understood the investment landscape, when she began to assess her own future life plans following the ordeal, she realised how little honesty and transparency there was in the investment industry. She knew a different approach was needed if people were to take their futures seriously.

She says, "When we're at the outset of our careers, starting families and enjoying our youth, the last thing we tend to think about is our mortality and how fragile life is – let alone how we're going to achieve the plans we may have for our retirement. Most of us, if we do imagine our future, we envisage travelling or taking up new passions and hobbies once we've completed our careers. However, without the right planning, things could be very different in reality.

"I wanted to offer a personal service. The Retail Distribution Review had recently introduced rules that promoted fairness in the industry, but my competitors seemed slow to change their ways."

Jillian used her savings to fund the launch and get her licence from the Financial Conduct Authority, which she needed to trade, within a few weeks – a process that can often take months. She recalls living on very little in the early days so that she could pay her staff: "I sometimes wondered why I had money in my purse when I didn't think I should have. It was only later that I learned my mum used to sneak in £50 here and there."

As a result of resigning from her employed role, Jillian was subject to a six-month non-competition clause. Once the time was up, however, her previous clients flocked to her new company. "This made the business sustainable and scalable, although the rapid growth meant we had to move address quickly. Our first office was at Renishaw Hall, which gave us credibility in the early days, however, our new premises had better IT provision and more space."

Marketing was vital to spreading the word about Jillian's approach to financial planning: "If people don't know about you, they can't buy your product! We used an external PR agency and promoted Future Life through social media, particularly on LinkedIn. We didn't pay to advertise; instead, we got in front of our customers by appearing at events and exhibitions. I was also president of the Sheffield Chamber of Commerce, which propelled me into the spotlight, both locally and nationally."

Future Life Wealth Management is now seen as one of the top financial planning firms in the UK; it has been in the *New Model Adviser*'s Top 100 since 2013. Jillian says, "We serve clients across the globe, thanks to some great back-office systems and web-based services. I was recently still able to help clients even while on a cruise between Sardinia and Sicily."

Jillian believes it's important to share the talents you hold with those around you. She describes herself as a "sponge", and says she loves soaking up knowledge from her team, her network and others. She also makes the distinction that she's a successful *professional* – a description that wouldn't change whatever her gender.

Explains Jillian, "I go wherever the business dictates and I have full confidence in my abilities." That's not to say the life of an entrepreneur is easy: "Because of client confidentiality, there's a lot I can't talk about. And even though I feel my gender doesn't impact the day-to-day work or the success of the business, it can be lonely being the only woman in the room. There are very few female IFAs in the industry – around 10% – and less than 2% of firms in the industry are wholly owned by women."

Clearly, 'trailblazer' is just another plaudit to add to Jillian's list. But what does she think of her success? "I felt getting my licence and launching my own brand was an unbeatable feeling, but now we're a few years down the line, I take greater satisfaction from playing a part in my team's development. I particularly like to see the younger members of staff grow in skills, experience and confidence," she says.

Jillian says she's always the "first one in the office and the last out". That's some commitment. Does she ever wind down? "I do feel I have a good work/life balance. I take regular holidays and strike the time out in the diary. I also clear space for regular reflexology, massage and hairdresser appointments – I keep these dates whatever happens with the business."

Boxing Day 2004 is a day many people – including Jillian – would probably prefer to forget, for various reasons.

But had the disaster not taken place, Jillian and Future Life Wealth Management might not be where they are now.

High:

"Winning my first award after being in business for just a year. It felt like confirmation I was doing everything right."

Low:

"I don't think I've had many lows – the tsunami helped me put everything into perspective, and I now find it easy to see positives everywhere. I can recall a couple of staff appointments that didn't work out, though, which had an impact on the business."

Golden nugget:

"If you don't have a good feeling about someone when you meet them for the first time, it's unlikely that feeling will go away at subsequent meetings. Just walk away."

Advice for others:

"Try and place yourself as the go-to and thought-leader expert in your field. I write columns and opinion pieces for my local paper and LinkedIn, and I'm often asked to comment on financial matters for BBC Breakfast, BBC 5 Live, Newsnight and others. I regularly speak on Radio Sheffield on all aspects of the economy and financial planning. It raises your profile and boosts your credibility."

20
BUILDING A BUSINESS IN FREIGHT AND TRANSPORT MANAGEMENT

Treat all people with respect, regardless of their role or position

Vicki Davenport – The Pink Link Ltd

Launching a business is hard, but driving change forward when you're a woman in a man's world is especially tough. Vicki Davenport is a stalwart of the logistics industry, and her company, The Pink Link Ltd, has forged its own path in this hugely competitive sector.

The company specialises in the distribution of small quantities of palletised freight, and runs a fleet of 20 vehicles throughout the UK and Europe. Years ago, it was one of the founding members of Palletways UK, which currently has

106 UK members and 350 across Europe. The Pink Link Ltd remains a Palletways UK Platinum Member, a rare accolade given to companies that deliver the highest standard of service possible against a range of key performance indicators.

So, how did Vicki and her team get to where they are today? She explains: "Originally, the company was called 'SBH Express Parcels'. Due to its financial difficulties and debt of a quarter of a million, the company was acquired by my father in 1991 for £1. He gave the business some capital to work with, and as its new sales director, I set about turning it around. Luckily, the company already had a loyal customer base and hard-working staff.

"Palletised distribution was a new concept at that time. The mainstream haulage companies were struggling to distribute deliveries of a few pallets at a competitive rate, and that's where we saw a gap in the market. The 'pallet network concept' soon became the preferred choice for this type of delivery. Palletways UK is now the market leader, handling 30,000 pallets every single night."

Once The Pink Link Ltd became associated with Palletways UK, it soon became apparent that the fleet of small transit vans they'd inherited needed upgrading to larger curtain-sided vehicles. They also needed some 18-tonne vehicles and a few articulated lorries. Acquiring these assets required serious capital investment; it also gave the company the perfect opportunity to rebrand.

Says Vicki, "We changed the baby-pink branding to the vibrant pink you see on the roads today. To maximise the rebrand, we used the services of a PR company. We also aligned with breast-cancer charities – a decision that stemmed from personal experience. To date, £160k of the £226k we've raised for charities since 2001 has been for breast-cancer care.

"Involvement with various charities has naturally brought marketing and promotional opportunities. Customers have told us they like the fact they're dealing with a company that has a strong, ethical, corporate social responsibility ethos."

Key milestones in The Pink Link Ltd's incredible journey include the moment Vicki and her brother, who subsequently joined the company, bought their father out in 2003/4.

Around that time, the company also won its first major award: Kirklees' Business of the Year. "That same week, we had a potential new client referred to us who distributed greeting cards nationwide. I sold them the concept of weekly palletised distribution, and they came on board. Over the next 12 years, this client grew from supplying 70 stores to over 880 stores, and we've been their key supplier throughout."

Though these events contributed significantly to the growth of Vicki's company, she made additional steps towards maximising profitability: "Our pallet services proved much more lucrative than the parcel-delivery side of the business. I began the process of shedding the parcel element, which represented 20% of the business when I put the plans in place. Before long, I'd managed to extricate it from our offering without losing a single client. I also made the choice to cull clients that were continual late-payers, or those who were unprofitable to us. All of this led to an excellent foundation for further growth, without the need for more staff. It was simply a case of working smarter, not harder."

Various software packages help Vicki to keep the business agile and efficient. "You have to constantly look at what's new on the market when it comes to IT so you can remain ahead of your competitors. When I started in this industry in 1983, the postcode system wasn't robust, and there were no satnavs! Today, everything is routed within a two-hour window, and reports can be produced at the push of a button. We've always invested heavily in our systems, which has given us a massive USP [unique selling point] over the years."

Pressures within the business include fluctuating fuel costs and sufficient staff numbers at peak time. Says Vicki, "The peak in transport begins in September as shops everywhere stock up for Christmas. None of our staff books their holiday entitlement during the last two months of the year, and we resist making any major changes during that time – it really is all hands on deck flat-out until Christmas Eve."

Perhaps unsurprisingly, the financial crash and subsequent recession proved a difficult time for the business: "Things were tough, and our prices stood still for several years. In 2014, we incorporated our first rate increase for six years; thankfully, it was well received by clients."

Does Vicki enjoy being an entrepreneur? "That's not a term I apply to myself. The success of the company is down to sheer hard work and long hours by a fantastic team of people with the same ethos, which is to provide the best possible service to our customers. That we have such longstanding clients is testament to this.

"I do feel incredibly proud to have reached 25 years in business, however, and I can't deny that I burst with pride every time I pass a Pink Link vehicle on the road. It's not been easy, though – for example, in the early days, I know I was was naïve and lacked experience. I struggled when asking clients to pay. Now, I believe that if you provide a good service the customer is happy with, you have every right to ask for your money and to be paid on time. You wouldn't go into a supermarket and walk out without paying, would you?

"My father taught me that turnover is vanity, profit is sanity – and you only ever run out of cash once. It took a while for me to understand this, but for me, it meant selling a service at a decent margin – not 'pile it high, sell it cheap'. That only leads to busy fools and a lack of money. My own motto is to treat all people with respect, regardless of their role or position."

As for Vicki's daily routine, it has changed over the years. For the first 20 years, she admits to working 12-hour days, juggling childcare around the commitments of the business. Back then, she found 5am on a Saturday morning the optimum window for catching up on things. Nowadays, her routine is more akin to the typical working day, although she still puts in more hours when necessary. "Many of my staff work long hours, and you have to lead by example," she says.

Vicki finds exercise an effective stress-reliever. "I play squash, go running, cycle and, more recently, I've got into yoga. Physical exertion is a great way to let off steam. I'm so busy during the day that I don't really get time to think about my stress levels, but one thing I do see as a challenge when you run your own business is how difficult it is to switch off. Today's technology means you're in constant contact, so I try not to look at my phone after 9pm. And if I'm on holiday, I only log in once a day; the management structure I have in place takes care of the daily routine."

High:

"It was amazing enough to get through to the final few, but to win an Inspiring Leader award in 2016 was unbelievable, as there were so many talented, successful women in the room."

Low:

"Hindsight is a wonderful thing. I like to think I've learnt from all the decisions I've made over the years, good and bad."

Golden nugget:

"If an opportunity sounds too good to be true, it usually is – so be careful not to jump in feet first without doing your homework. I once took a phone call from a prospective client who asked me to collect 10 pallets that day (which is unusual; customers rarely change their logistics supplier on the back of a phone call – it usually involves weeks of meetings and negotiations). My sales manager thought it was a great opportunity and couldn't understand why I was holding back… but after a couple of hours spent checking the company's credentials, we found they'd been unable to pay their existing supplier, who'd put their account on hold. We politely declined their business."

Advice for others:

"When I started out, logistics was a male-dominated environment, and I'm delighted to see more and more women in the sector now. One piece of advice I'd give to anyone seeking a career in logistics is that it's a very competitive industry; you will need determination as well as the ability to communicate at all levels to succeed."

21
CREATE A USER EXPERIENCE AGENCY

Feel the fear and do it anyway

Lisa Duddington (Ortega) – Keep It Usable

Lisa Duddington's journey is nothing short of amazing. Despite knowing she had a unique solution that filled a gap in the market, her early attempts to get Keep It Usable off the ground were hampered because no one really knew what she was offering. She recalls: "People just didn't understand what we did, as it was so unusual and unique. This made applying for initial funding difficult. For example, we went for a £150 grant and lost out to a man whose business idea was hand-delivering leaflets. It would have been very easy to forget the whole idea and call everything off."

A user experience (UX) agency, Keep It Usable uses psychology, research and behavioural science to design services and products for their clients. Much of the agency's work is centred on digital user experiences such as websites, apps and software. The team spends a lot of time uncovering how people think, feel and behave before translating its findings into concepts and designs that persuade customers to act.

Before launching the business, Lisa was a UX and usability specialist for Sony Ericsson. She was good at her work – so good that colleagues often commented that she should set up her own agency. She spent a couple of years designing and building a social network before returning to the idea. As she says, "All I had to do was set up the business and get clients!"

Working in the UX industry had shown Lisa that her competitors tended to be either a design agency or a research agency. Few outside of London brought the two specialisms together, and even fewer based their concepts on customer insights and a deep understanding of human psychology and behaviour. Lisa wanted to show clients that designs were infinitely more successful when they met both the needs of a client's business and those of the end user. She also wanted to offer more transparency – a trait she felt was severely lacking in her industry.

She says, "When I was at Sony Ericsson, I became increasingly frustrated with the agencies they used. "I wanted to build an agency based on trust and openness, where the client only worked with senior UX professionals and could expect the highest-quality work at a much lower cost than our competitors in the capital."

Lisa built the business from nothing. "We'd already lived off beans on toast and 9p noodles from Asda, so we were used to surviving on very little!" Fortunately, it wasn't long before the company secured a contract. Lisa then invested the income from that project towards finding others.

As you can imagine, traditional marketing doesn't work for a business like Keep It Usable. Because trust is such an integral part of their offering, word of mouth has always been key for the company, however, it has taken a long time to gather a sizeable client base and to instil themselves in customers' minds as experts in the industry.

Keep It Usable's first major client was Manchester Council, who sought the agency's help to overhaul their website into something more user-centric. Lisa says, "This was a radical move on their part, as council websites tended to follow an established layout. We won the work over a competitor, who were unhappy with the decision – this gave us a huge confidence boost. We tested our concept of the site with local residents and advised the council on necessary changes to improve usability during the test stages.

"The end result proved a success, and it even went on to win awards. This generated a good amount of publicity, which saw other councils and companies approach us. Manchester Council's success inspired us to submit examples of our work to other awards bodies, and we won! This also helped us to be noticed by our target clients and served as further proof that we were good at what we did."

Lisa's reputation as an expert has been boosted by appearances in the media, and the talks she's often asked to give. "I used to dislike public speaking, but I'd agree anyway," she says. "The surprising thing is that I actually began to enjoy it, and it turns out that I'm pretty good at it, too. Each invitation to speak would lead to more – then, through Twitter, the BBC found me. They invited me onto BBC Breakfast, which is live, as a 'tech expert', to discuss why we're all addicted to our digital devices. They didn't ask me any of the questions they said they were going to ask (and which I'd prepared for); despite my calm exterior, I was absolutely panicking inside! Thankfully, the appearance went well. Afterwards, I thought, 'I can handle live TV – nothing can ever be as scary as that.' I really believe we need to push ourselves out of our comfort zones to discover exactly what we're capable of."

Having worked in a corporate environment before becoming an entrepreneur, Lisa found some aspects of being a business owner different to how she'd imagined them. "You spend most of your time not doing the thing you love, but everything else necessary to make the business run – such as the accounts, marketing, sales, HR, etc. You have to learn to like the business side just as much, if not more, than the other aspects of setting up a company, or find the means to outsource these elements."

Lisa and her team use Apple Macbooks. She believes that although they're more expensive than other computers, they are worth the investment because they "last longer and create fewer headaches". She also says eye-tracking technology [a device for measuring eye movement and positions] is crucial, because "It enables the team to see what people are looking at online and how they interact with software".

She admits she was money-driven in the early days, but today values the freedom and choice success has brought far more. "The variety of opportunities running your own business can bring can be worth more than money. Had I remained an employee, there's no way I'd be the person I am today."

She hasn't always trusted her instincts, though, which led to a poor business decision. "I was conscious when I first started out that I lacked business knowledge, having never sold a thing in my life. The idea of selling didn't appeal to me at all, so I thought it was best to leave this to someone who knew what they were doing. I eventually realised I was the best person to sell my business's services as I had the expertise and skills in UX. I had the knowledge and case-study examples – and most importantly, I had passion. Don't waste time with mentors, coaches and business development people – the owners are the best people to sell a business."

Lisa says Susan Jeffers' book *Feel the Fear and Do It Anyway* helped her to take risks and try new things. "Taking action is what's important. Don't assume you have to have huge reserves of confidence before you can do anything. It actually works the other way around: if do what you fear, it's this that builds your confidence and stretches your abilities."

Lisa sticks to a schedule to achieve balance. "There are only 24 hours in each day, so you have to exercise discipline in some areas. Unfortunately, your social life tends to fall by the wayside when you run your own business." She continually tweaks her daily routine to get the best from her time, waking around 6.30am and then taking the 20-minute walk to the office. "I spend this time thinking of three things I'm grateful for, which puts me in a positive frame of mind for the day ahead. I tend to eat breakfast at the office.

After checking her social media feeds, it's on to client meetings and the creation of proposals. Sometimes she's hands-on, and spends time researching. At lunchtime she makes sure she takes time away from the computer in favour of fresh air before spending the afternoon writing and negotiating. At home she unwinds with Yin or Ashtanga yoga, and she loves to do creative things such as reading or writing.

More recently, Lisa has begun to incorporate mindfulness into her life. After learning that a lot of business leaders practise meditation, Lisa took a couple of courses to learn more. Before bed Lisa spends a few minutes meditating, which helps to relax her mind. If she still has trouble drifting off, she uses the Calm app. "I love their stories. I can't make it past five minutes without falling asleep!"

High:

Realising that I can handle live TV after an initial fear of public speaking. I've been invited onto BBC Breakfast as a 'tech expert', to discuss why we're all addicted to our digital devices.

Low:

"Employ the right people. I spent two years mentoring and training someone, even though they simply weren't suitable. I was blinded by my faith in them and I should have dismissed them much sooner."

Golden nugget:

"Focus on profit. Some business owners focus on the wrong figures. Revenue means nothing if your expenses are so high you're making little profit. Having a big team means nothing if you struggle to pay their wages every month. Having a grand office means nothing if you find it difficult to pay the rent."

Advice for others:

"The only person you can fully rely on is yourself. Treat yourself like you would your best friend – speak kindly to yourself, be positive, push yourself forwards and tell yourself you can do it! Reward yourself when you hit targets, and remember to take time out. Sometimes your best ideas come when you take a step back."

22
FRANCHISE YOUR EXPERTISE AND BUILD A BUSINESS AROUND IT

The harder you work, the luckier you get

Caroline Sparks – Turtle Tots

Caroline Sparks runs the baby and toddler swimming business, Turtle Tots, with her business partner, Gabrielle Lixton. It is no hobby, though – it now has numerous franchisees across the UK and Ireland.

Gabrielle first created the Turtle Tots programme in 2010 as a seamless and fun journey that starts with aqua-natal yoga for mums-to-be and continues with baby and toddler swimming lessons. Since drowning is the third most common cause of accidental infants' deaths worldwide, both Caroline and Gaby are proud to play their part in reducing this statistic. Caroline and Gaby's mission is to create lessons that are great fun and enjoyable, but the overall mission is to teach an important skill that may save a life one day.

Initially, Gaby launched Turtle Tots lessons in Bristol, but demand quickly outstripped supply. She realised how scalable the business could be and how potentially lucrative it was, but knew she needed help to get it off the ground.

Once Caroline came on board, the pair researched the swimming market extensively, finding a gap between cheap-and-cheerful basic lessons in leisure centres and more expensive lessons run by their franchisor competitors. Together, they launched Turtle Tots with limited savings and credit card funds. "We wanted to create a fun, friendly, aspirational brand that came at an affordable price," says Caroline. "Franchising was a large part of our business plan; we felt Turtle Tots would appeal to people looking for a flexible, rewarding business. By January 2017, we were teaching 10,000 students each week – a mix of expectant mothers, babies and toddlers."

Introducing 'Bubble' – the duo's bespoke business-management software – in 2014 made a huge difference to the business. The software allowed customers to book classes online, view/order underwater photos of their children and buy Turtle Tots' branded products through the website. This streamlined day-to-day operations. The program also helped licensees manage their own businesses more effectively – they could run reports, and access marketing materials and other documents in the Turtle Tots' online library. As technology moved on, Bubble was superseded by an even better software system in 2020.

In 2017, there was an opportunity to bolster the brand's unique offering. Caroline explains: "The Swimming Teachers' Association introduced the Level 3 Diploma in Baby and Pre-School teaching. The qualification built on research into child psychology and neuroscience and was aimed at experienced swimming teachers. Rather than ignore it, we committed to making sure every eligible teacher passed the new qualification. This gave our brand even more credibility, and parents had the confidence to know they were engaging a programme that incorporated the latest advice and techniques."

While Caroline and Gaby don't label themselves as entrepreneurs, Caroline cites the flexibility of being able to look after her own family while doing something she enjoyed as the reason she threw everything towards making Turtle Tots a success. She remembers how it felt when they recruited their first franchisee and how exciting it was to exceed their forecasts, but says, "Nowadays, though, success is the knowledge that we have over 250 franchisees, teachers and staff are doing fun, flexible, rewarding jobs they love."

Her favourite motto is "the harder you work, the luckier you get". Although she thinks those around her would call her competitive, she prefers to be called 'driven'. She does the school run before heading to the gym each morning; once in work, she spends a lot of time in meetings, or consulting suppliers and meeting potential franchisees. Between appointments, she may write award applications or deal with franchisee renewals.

So, how does she manage to remain focused and grounded? "Having a business partner definitely alleviates stress. We're each other's sounding board if any issues arise, and we can bounce pros and cons around before we make a decision."

Caroline also has a great support network at home, being married and having two teenagers. She never takes for granted all she has. "I absolutely love my job," she says, "and I feel incredibly fortunate to be one of the co-founders of Turtle Tots – it's wonderful working with Gaby and such a great team, and with so many amazing franchisees and teachers. Our vision is to teach 30,000 babies and toddlers a week by 2022, and be recognised as the best baby-and-toddler swim school in the UK."

High:

"In 2015, Turtle Tots won the Hewlett Packard Export Award run by Enterprise Nation. We won places on a trade mission to Shanghai. Along with 40 other entrepreneurs, we enjoyed an inspirational few days, which involved meeting the UK Minister for Trade and finding out the intricacies of launching a business in China. This led to a meeting at 10 Downing Street, chaired by the Prime Minister."

Low:

"I wish we'd known about Research and Development (R&D) tax credits earlier. I'd heard about them, but until 2017, I hadn't realised we would qualify. Every business owner should ask their accountant about these, or a specialist R&D lawyer – they may be entitled to them."

Golden nugget:

"Don't confuse activity with progress. It's easy to be a busy fool. And don't chase profits – chase happy customers and the profits will come naturally. The thousands of parents that bring their babies and toddlers to our classes every week are advocates of our brand, simply because they love what we do."

Advice to others:

"Networking is invaluable. It's an opportunity to talk over issues with like-minded people who can give sound advice – many have been in your shoes at some point."

23
START YOUR OWN ENGINEERING COMPANY

Decide to be a change-maker

Roni Savage – Jomas Associates Ltd

Roni Savage's mission was clear: she wanted to break the mould and become a female CEO in the male-dominated engineering industry she knew so well. "I decided I wanted to be a change-maker," she says.

After graduating with a degree in Engineering Geology and Geotechnics, and subsequently completing an MSc in Environmental Management, Roni enjoyed a successful career as an engineering geologist, working for various consultancies across the UK. She was even headhunted in 2006 and offered the position of associate director for one of the country's largest engineering companies.

Her ambition – to run her own engineering company and make it a huge success – began when she launched Jomas

Associates (Engineering & Environmental) Ltd. She planned to use a different approach to the one many of her peers had adopted, which involved being client- and value-focused while also being strategic and pragmatic, bearing in mind many of her clients were under time pressures for delivery.

Jomas Associates undertakes site investigations, land-contamination risk assessments, and geotechnical investigations to facilitate construction projects across the UK. Clients come from all sectors: residential, industrial, commercial land development and government bodies, as well as schools and hospitals.

Says Roni: "The population in the UK is increasing and the country is currently facing a housing crisis. Land development is required to meet the demand – not just for housing, but also for the surrounding infrastructure: roads, retail outlets, schools, etc. The assessment of ground conditions is critical if a project is to be successful. With very few green sites for development, there's a real need to reclaim brownfield and derelict sites. My intention when I started the company was that Jomas would provide the expertise to make this process easier, which I saw as a real gap in the market."

Roni used her savings to fund the launch, and the company went on to realise £200k in its first year – a figure that was four times her target. She knew then that the company had the potential for growth. Even though this would have been enough for most people, she found the time and energy to launch a second company – Turner-

Jomas, a multi-disciplinary civil engineering practice. This brought Roni further opportunities to scale up.

So, what has helped Jomas grow by 30% year on year? "Networking, networking and more networking!" Roni admits. "Jomas is built on our ability to forge strong relationships, deliver a great service and be subsequently referred to new clients. This was my vision – I knew customer service was critical to Jomas's growth. I take clients' deadlines into account and focus on the delivery – it's this approach that's seen the business thrive."

A tipping point arrived when Roni knew she needed staff to help her cope with the workload. At the same time, she moved the company into more permanent business premises. "This really changed things. I had to acknowledge that I had a 'true' business and that failure was not an option. The hardest part was ensuring I had a workforce that understood Jomas's strategy, vision and values. It's hard work building a business; bringing the right people along with you is critical to its success. I am extremely proud of my team at Jomas, as they are committed to the excellence that underpins all of our work."

A proud mum of three boys, Roni no doubt has excellent organisational and negotiating skills. Running her own business looks as if it's always been on the cards. Is the experience everything she thought it would be? "I had no expectations when I started Jomas, and I don't particularly think of myself as an entrepreneur. One thing I will say is that it's not as easy as some people may believe. Not everyone would suit being their own boss either, however attractive the thought may be when you feel stuck in your job or career. It's not the easy way out. There's a lot to be said for leaving your employer's premises for the day, knowing you don't have to think about your job until the next time you're there. As a business owner, you never switch off.

"My view of an entrepreneur is someone who creates a business to enforce change, not someone who's doing it just to make money. It's a question of purpose and priorities. So, maybe I am an entrepreneur after all. I enjoy running Jomas, but it is certainly not without its challenges."

Roni credits the company's bespoke project-management system as a crucial element in the efficiency of the business. She says she's lucky in that she wouldn't change what she's implemented over the course of Jomas's history. She has simply focused on providing a high-quality, high-value service, and success has followed.

Says Roni, "When I started the business, success meant earning enough to pay my bills while allowing me to spend time with my kids. Now that the company has achieved as much as it has, and because I have a good team around me to take some of the strain off me, I can spend more time working 'on' the business than 'in' it. Today, success means making a difference in the industry, while scaling up and making the Jomas name into a brand that will be remembered for a very long time."

Roni is also a mum, so it's easy to imagine her daily routine and the types of jobs she still has to do, regardless of the fact she's one of few female CEOs in a male-dominated industry. These include getting the kids up for school, doing the school run, helping with homework and chauffeuring them to their various activities. Downtime can be hard to come by: "A good cuppa and some trashy TV helps me to wind down and chill out. That said, there's no better stress relief than a hug from my boys."

High:

"Taking Jomas to a turnover of £2m – a key milestone the business hit in 2017, which was the same year I took part in the Goldman Sachs' Small Business Programme. I now think a lot bigger than I did, and I believe we can reach £10m with a strategic plan. Ultimately, I've found that the better we do, the bigger I think."

Low:

"Recruiting emotionally. I've learned that the most important thing when hiring someone is not how much you like them, but how well they can do the job."

Golden nugget:

"Work hard, believe in yourself, and grab every opportunity with two hands and two legs!"

Advice for others:

"Find a mentor or buddy you can bounce ideas off. How can you ever know if your thoughts and plans are sound if only *you* get to know about them?"

GOLDEN RULES FOR SCALING UP

As you can see from the stories, scaling up a venture is not for the faint-hearted. It requires strong leadership and the vision to be able to take a business from start-up to a mature and thriving enterprise. The women who thrive at this stage of a business's life cycle are those who can evolve and are committed to developing the skills needed to lead their companies through the turbulence and pains associated with this phase.

Here is a summary of the top tips for women in the scale-up phase of their journey.

1. Get a mentor

Through mentoring and positive role modelling you can be inspired and supported to scale your business to heights that were previously unimaginable. If you are looking to scale your business, then find yourself a business mentor who has done it – preferably one already working in the type of business you are looking to scale. Having a sounding board for your ideas is invaluable. Why make your own mistakes when you can learn from other people's mistakes?

2. Invest in your people

Be confident enough in your own abilities to surround yourself with excellent people and to invest in their development because you can't build a thriving enterprise on your own.

3. Pick star players and coach them

Recruitment should not be an emotional affair. The most important thing when hiring someone is not how much you like them, but how well they can do the job and how great a team player they are. Treat people fairly and consistently. Once you understand that no one is better or worse than anyone else, it's much easier to lead with empathy as everything in business involves people.

4. Focus on profitability

Some business owners focus on the wrong figures. Revenue means nothing if your expenses are so high you're making little profit. Having a big team means nothing if you struggle to pay their wages every month. Having a grand office means nothing if you find it difficult to pay the rent. Try not to get lost in the ego-driven metrics and don't confuse activity with progress. It is very easy to be a busy fool.

5. Focus on culture and ethics

It's difficult to change the ethics and culture of your company, so start as you mean to go on. Engage with your team, model behaviours and language that you want to amplify. Work is not always only about work. A small break from work pressures improves productivity – so take breaks, have fun and allow your team the breaks they need to thrive. If you create a positive and empowering culture in your business, this will be reflected externally to your clients.

6. Take calculated risks

Risk is something you're bound to encounter as an entrepreneur. Take as many of the informed, calculated risks that you can, as this will grow your business. Do your homework and research your market, as well as learn from any mistakes. Make no assumptions about deals – they could go either way.

7. Focus on building your network and investing in long-term relationships

Remember that people buy from people they know and like. Learn the skills you need to be able to nurture long-term relationships if these skills do not come naturally to you. To be honest, few people enjoy attending networking events or speaking to strangers. It is one of these areas where you must recognise the value a network brings to your professional life and business, then invest the time to make it happen. Aim always to leave people better than you found them.

8. Think big

Opportunities come and go. To scale your business, you need to be able to think big; take advantage of opportunities that will make those big dreams a reality. If you are going to negotiate a deal, then why not x10 the deal – it might take the same amount of effort.

9. Build a personal brand

Position yourself as the go-to and thought-leader expert in your field. Write columns and opinion pieces for your local paper and on LinkedIn. It raises your profile and boosts your credibility and amplifies the "know, like and trust" factor.

10. Don't sweat the small stuff

We women can be hard on ourselves. It doesn't help that we are not always given the respect we deserve as businesswomen. This lack of respect can be to our advantage if we don't let it get to us – it gives as that element of surprise when we are underestimated. If you don't have a good feeling about someone or a deal at the first instance, don't talk yourself out of that feeling. It is unlikely that feeling will go away at subsequent meetings. Just walk away.

11. Have a plan

What are you trying to achieve in business? Is it to change an industry or simply making money? Most successful entrepreneurs are clear from day one on what they want to create. Spend time each week and month planning and reviewing the key numbers in your business. Create a dashboard that helps you to focus on the numbers that really matter to your business and industry and monitor your progress against your plan. That way, you will feel prepared and in control of all aspects of your businesses performance. Document things and remember your brain is not for storing information about your business processes – write everything down and clear your mind for creativity.

12. Be kind to yourself

Make time for breaks. Technology is there to serve us. Don't be a slave to your phone or computer. There is always something you could be working on when it comes to your business, but there are very few things that won't wait until the next day. Treat yourself like you would your best friend – speak kindly to yourself, be positive, push yourself forwards and tell yourself you can do it! Reward yourself when you hit targets, and remember to take time out. Sometimes your best ideas come when you take a step back.

SECTION 3:
MOVING ON: BECOMING AN ANGEL INVESTOR

Knowing when it's the right time to exit

Sometimes in life, things can get to a point where other issues begin to take priority over your business and career. Although it is never an easy decision to move on, it might be necessary due to life's changing circumstances.

Sometimes the excitement of building your business can begin to slow, and you suddenly find it does not give you the same level of fulfilment it did ten years ago when you first started. After running a successful business for a few years, many simply feel it is time to start a new chapter, to write a new story for their lives. This may mean either moving on to other exciting opportunities, or simply moving in a different direction.

Unfortunately, when you are a business owner, the option of changing course is not always available, and the decision to move on is not as straightforward as it would be for those in normal employment. Your business is not only your job; it is also an extension of yourself –your identity and lifestyle are inextricably linked to the nature of your business. But if the season changes and a new chapter needs to be written, then that call must be heeded.

Life is made of seasons. During some seasons, it makes sense to be up all night working, building and scaling your business. But during other seasons, it may be more appropriate to scale back and take a slower pace.

Some move on because they feel they have taken the business as far as their skills will take it, at which point it may be time to hand over the reins to someone else with the energy and enthusiasm to take the business to its next level of growth and development. Some exit their businesses by selling it on to others, thereby enabling them to retire, become angel investors or even start a fresh new venture after a period of rest. If there is no ready buyer for the business, it might also be necessary for them to wind down their business and ultimately shut it down, marking the full end of a cycle.

This section of the book focuses on stories of a few successful female entrepreneurs who started, scaled up and ultimately exited their businesses. Some of the women profiled here have taken the skills they have developed in running their businesses and are now helping others in growing their own business. These women are truly rare unicorns, because only 12% of venture capitalists or angel investors are women. We need more women with the economic power and disposable wealth who can invest in and support the future generation of female entrepreneurs.

24
BUILDING A GLOBAL COFFEE CHAIN BRAND

Leap, and the net will appear

Sahar Hashemi – Coffee Republic

While some entrepreneurs launch their businesses with an exit plan in mind, most have no idea where they will end up.

Sahar Hashemi is probably one of the more well-known contributors in this book; her first company, Coffee Republic, is recognisable as the ground-breaking, original chain of UK gourmet coffee outlets – the company that paved the way for other well-known coffee chains such as Starbucks, Caffé Nero and Costa Coffee.

In 1994, Sahar, a trained lawyer, spent some time in New York. There, she found the state had a rapidly growing thirst for luxurious lattes, creamy cappuccinos and energising espressos. When she returned to the UK, she was disappointed that the only coffee 'experience' she could find was straight-out-of-the kettle instant coffee served in a polystyrene cup.

Sahar says the death of her father in the previous year was what became the catalyst for her entrepreneurial journey, giving her the push to act: "The realisation that life is brief, and that we never know if we'll even be here tomorrow, gave me a lot to think about.

"Being a lawyer could sometimes feel like a punishment, and I wanted to have fun at work. I didn't feel fulfilled. I wanted to get up every morning looking forward to going to work, knowing I would love what I do when I got there. Where every day would be different, and I would be working towards a purpose. I needed a goal that would drive me. Creating Coffee Republic gave me all those things."

The following months were a blur of intensive market research, including her quest for the right physical site and securing capital investment. The following year, Sahar and her brother Bobby opened the first Coffee Republic outlet in London.

Sahar details their journey in her book *Anyone Can Do It* – a searingly honest account of the company's launch, growth and subsequent sale. It chronicles the story of her initial seed (or should that be coffee bean?) idea to the time she and Bobby bravely stepped down from their management roles in 2001, and ultimately reached the point where the chain had created around 100 outlets across the UK before they decided to exit and move on.

They say you know it is the right time to exit when the company is a fully fledged adult and no longer the baby you first nurtured, although that does not mean exiting is a painless experience. Sahar was on a flight back from the US the day the *Financial Times* broke the story of their departure from Coffee Republic. She says, "I found a copy in the airport lounge and [when I read it, I] burst into uncontrollable tears. The other passengers were aghast, and probably wondered what it was I had read that provoked such emotion."

Once the company's buyout was complete, Sahar had the financial freedom to retire. "While I could have simply stopped and enjoyed the fruits of my labour, perhaps becoming 'a lady that lunched', it didn't appeal to me. Though it may sound like utopia, I could not just sit around or shop all day. Bobby and I had had our noses to the grindstone for so long by then that it was difficult to find a reason to get up once it all ended. I just felt lost and empty. That's when I knew I had to find something else just as fulfilling."

That was when she wrote *Anyone Can Do It*. "I found the process of writing incredibly therapeutic. The time flew by when we were building the brand; putting it down on paper helped me see what we did well and what lessons we learned. It gave me the opportunity to relive the whole journey, which was cathartic as we didn't get time to enjoy it while it was happening." She also decided to launch a new company – Skinny Candy, a brand that sells low-sugar, low-fat confectionery.

Fast-forward to today, and Sahar has also committed her time to working a few days a week for the social enterprise Change Please – a coffee company that helps the homeless, pays fair wages to farmers across the globe and supports a range of causes, such as the victims of domestic abuse – alongside other senior executives from Starbucks, Pret a Manger and Jimmy Choo. Says Sahar, "I feel it's important to give back whatever and whenever we can. I have learned so much since starting my first business – and if there is a chance I can help someone else by sharing what I know, that is what I want to do. It also gives my life what I felt it missed after Coffee Republic: a purpose."

Giving back has also seen Sahar co-chairing the government's Scale-Up Taskforce. She gives talks within larger companies on the subject of entrepreneurship, and works with business ambassadors like Nick Jenkins, founder of Moonpig, and Emma Jones of Enterprise Nation. She also generously gives her time to sit on the advisory board of forwardladies.com.

Surely she's just as busy as before? Says Sahar, "Once you work at a higher level, it's hard to stop. You get used to fitting a lot into your day. It's a mindset – we all have 24 hours, it's what you do with them that counts. It's also about choosing the right opportunities. My inbox is often flooded with various offers and proposals, but I don't want to just do *anything*. I like to I know that I'm making a real contribution."

Sahar is a firm believer in the law of attraction: "I think it's true that thoughts become things. You've got to put yourself out there, know what you want and have faith that it will happen. Once you know what the end goal is, the universe will present opportunities and ways for you to get there. What it can't do is make you act – only you can do that.

"Successful women are still seen as an anomaly, but you have to carve a life out for yourself. You can't rely on anyone else or look to your husband to provide everything. When I began Coffee Republic, I just wanted to enjoy my work; making money was a nice side-effect. That said, I did have a plan – I wanted to create a nationwide chain of coffee shops. Bobby and I made that happen."

Sahar admits she didn't really know what an entrepreneur was when she first started out, so she had no expectations: "It wasn't a well-used term back then. Of course, I'm grateful for everything I've achieved, but the definition of success has never changed for me. Though I like nice things and can be materialistic at times, true success is having the freedom to do what I love. The feeling that work is so much fun it's practically a hobby – something I could happily do until the day I die."

Gratitude also plays an important part in Sahar's life. "I use Tim Ferriss's app, the Five-Minute Journal. It puts you in a positive mindset. I find it much better than idling time away on social media, which can be disruptive – it can also make you critical of yourself and your own success because it's too easy to compare it to the apparent success of others."

Most days, Sahar works from home, but even when she does, she makes a 'faux commute': "The first thing I do each morning is drive to the park to walk the dog. There's something about that action that sets me up for the day. It would be so easy to roll out of bed and sit at my desk; driving back from the park feels like I'm commuting to my place of work. It's really important to me to have a strict divide between work and home. When my husband walks in from his job, I don't want to still be working. When he comes home, that's the working day over; it's our time then. I've never struggled to find 'me' time either, as I know how important it is to look after yourself. I strive to eat well, as I believe food can have a huge impact on how we perform. I exercise regularly and spend a few minutes each day meditating.

"Technology has its place in my life, but only to make it easier. I love Google Keep – it's the best to-do-list service I've come across. The others remove a task once you've completed it, as if it never existed, so you can feel as if you constantly have loads to do. I take great satisfaction from seeing items crossed off in Keep – they remind me of what I've achieved that day!"

Having built and sold a hugely successful business, and with people queuing up to know what she knows, Sahar's life looks charmed from the outside. Does she have any regrets? "I do. A very big one: I wish I'd not sold Coffee Republic. You only have one amazing business in your lifetime, and that was mine. It was such an amazing experience and I really miss it." A common saying is that business isn't personal, but Sahar's story suggests otherwise.

High:

"Coming home to a letter from the Cabinet Office saying that I'd been awarded an OBE from the Queen. Hearing that *Anyone Can Do It* has inspired someone to start their own journey towards success. The biggest high for me, however, was the simple act of having a coffee in my own coffee shop."

Low:

"Selling Coffee Republic!"

Golden nugget:

"My parents drilled into us that 'You can only do your best and God does the rest'. Ask yourself as you get up every morning: What's the best I can do today?"

Advice for others:

"Leap, and the net will appear. Just do something – it's far worse not to act. Also, if you're thinking about exiting your business, don't make any rash decisions, however tired you are or how much you think you want rid of it. Don't cut yourself off completely, because when it's gone, it's gone.

"Once you know what the end goal is, the universe will present opportunities and ways for you to get there. What it can't do is make you act – only you can do that."

25
BUILDING BUSINESSES WITH PURPOSE

Empowering others as a driver: what have you got to lose?

Rachel Hannan – Angel Investor

By the time Rachel Hannan made her first 'Angel Investment', she'd already worked her way up the career ladder as a managing consultant in PwC and gone on to found 2 businesses herself. As someone who is passionate about learning, trying new things and inspiring others, starting a business – not just working in someone else's – seemed like a logical next step.

With previous experience of a start-up, having been heavily involved in launching her then-partner's manufacturing firm, Rachel had managed several areas of the business, ranging from accounts and payroll to marketing and HR. Despite the challenges of fitting this around her corporate career, she found she enjoyed the challenge of a small enterprise, and even put her entire savings into the company's growth. It was her first taste of risk and reward, and by the time she exited the business the investment she'd originally made had increased four-fold.

Later, but still enjoying her role at PwC, she faced a choice when they sold the practice she worked within. It proved to be a catalyst and one that set her on an exciting next chapter. Rachel made the decision to leave the corporate world and with a business partner launched GatenbySanderson – a specialist recruitment firm for senior public sector appointments.

Rachel felt she had a good range of skills and experience to apply to a new venture, which proved to be true when the business became a leader in its field. Though the company had much larger competitors, GatenbySanderson gained a reputation for providing a truly excellent service. She says, "A core driver for me was that I felt the competition had become complacent; big companies resting on their laurels. I wanted to offer something different, better. I was motivated by the fact the people in the roles we recruited for had a massive impact on society, designing and delivering services that could really make an impact on individuals and communities, so we had to get it right."

The plan with GatenbySanderson was clear: launch, build, expand, sustain, then exit. Rachel never doubted that it would be scalable. Within eight years, and when Rachel sold her stake in the company, it was turning over £24m, with a pre-tax profit of more than £4m. Having been focused, driven and goal-orientated for so long, exiting meant Rachel felt directionless for the first time. She'd already learned so much from her involvement on the front line, in management and in the boardroom. How could she apply all of that to something new, and what would that be?

This was in 2010. The 2008 financial crisis still loomed large and the economy was struggling. Rachel remembers the headlines of the time: Unemployment up! Economic stagnation, banks not lending, youth unemployment at significant levels, businesses struggling. "That's when I became interested in angel investment," she says. "It wasn't just about giving a business a financial boost – I felt I could bring a lot more to the table. I could mentor and advise. Although some of my fellow angels had been investing much longer than I had, I had recent, first-hand experience of the pressures, constraints and specific challenges within a business. I could also see the bigger picture: if the business was successful, it would create jobs; this in turn would help the economy and give those struggling a new sense of purpose. Empowering others was a real driver for me to invest my money."

Rachel had the means, the experience and the desire to give growing businesses a boost. What she lacked in the early days, however, was confidence: "There was part of me that thought, 'Can I do this, will I be seen as credible?' My fellow investors had gone through the process a number of times, and though I knew I had an array of useful skills and knowledge, it was a whole new area for me."

Rachel did her homework and initially chose to invest as part of a syndicate, initially starting with conservative amounts before increasing her investment's size and often later as a solo investor. She helped businesses across a range of sectors, including education, technology, medical devices and food manufacturing. "It was hugely inspiring to know I was playing a part in another business's success, and I began to trust my gut instincts more and more."

When Rachel became an angel investor, there was a severe lack of women doing the same. "Ten years ago, only around 9% of angel investors were women nationally, and at the time probably less in Yorkshire. Now, it's nearer 14%, which is better, but there needs to be more. Women make good business leaders and natural entrepreneurs, and women investors are more likely to back women entrepreneurs. We know how to juggle priorities and tend to think more creatively; we're naturally good problem-solvers. Female entrepreneurs get the best out of others – they make things happen, they collaborate well, they're good communicators and they're incredibly resilient."

Having seen the corporate world and the business world from a variety of angles, Rachel found she enjoyed being an angel – something she fits around the numerous other roles she holds, including mentoring, advisory work, being on the board of a number of companies and other organisations and working with charities. She gives a significant amount of time free of charge. "It's great to be in a position to give back. I get so much out of it, too. I learn something new all the time."

Rachel describes herself as being very driven – a workaholic, even. Though she may mix with some high-powered people, she remains down-to-earth, honest and decidedly realistic. She admits, "There's no way I would have got where I am today if I thought 'having it all' was achievable. For me personally I don't think it is.

"I really do admire the businesswomen who juggle all areas well – and there are plenty of them.

However, I think there are as many women who feel a failure if they're not 'perfect' on both sides of the fence. Remember: our expectations are usually self-imposed, and not all of them serve us well."

Rachel cites the ability to spot opportunities, take risks, sheer hard work and a dose of luck as the formula for her success: "I know women who have worked just as hard as I have, with the same dedication and commitment, who could have gone further than me given exposure to the right opportunities. If that hasn't happened, it isn't a fault of theirs, it's just life and the way it unfolds. For example, the opportunity to have a family didn't present itself to me, but I make the most of the cards I've been dealt.

"I'm not someone who has unlimited innate confidence. I have to work at it. Confidence is like kryptonite for some women, and yet we have so many transferable skills and marketable qualities. Things began to change when I stopped asking myself, 'Can I do that?' and started to ask, 'Why do I assume someone else would do it better?' I have experience across all areas: corporate, advisory, finance, business growth, leadership, management, people … why wouldn't I be a great asset in helping others grow their business? Once I realised what I had to offer, I never looked back."

To date, Rachel has invested well into seven figures in start-ups and growing businesses. She says, "It's more common for investors to lose their money than to make it, but when investments do go well, it 'hopefully' more than makes up for the other losses! Rachel has recently added funding house building to her activities, particularly the creation of new starter homes on brown field sites. It's an industry she's enjoyed learning more about. "This is key. I always ask myself three questions when I look at an investment proposal: 1) Is it worthwhile/will it make a difference? 2) Will it challenge me/will I enjoy it? And lastly, 3) Is it commercially viable?!"

When someone has achieved so much, what else is there to aspire to? "That's a good question," she says. "I sit on a variety of regional boards, but I'd like to progress this to organisations on a national level. I'd also like to expand my work as an angel to larger businesses; sometimes, these can need more help and advice than start-ups as they really scale. Not every new business will be another Amazon, but it doesn't mean they're not attractive or viable."

Rachel doesn't sound like someone who has an issue with stress. Is that just an assumption? "I admit I perhaps have a higher tolerance to stress than some people, but I don't think anyone has absolutely no stress in their life. I'm very good at switching off – not necessarily on a day-to-day basis, but when I'm on holiday, I'm on holiday! But I'm the first to admit I need to make more time for non-work related activities!

"I don't exercise extravagance and live much as I did ten years ago, although I have made time to get married now – is that an extravagance?! I enjoy the simple things in life, but will splurge occasionally on a really nice holiday. But what I have gained through my success is the freedom to do what I choose, which is invaluable. I probably don't exercise it as much as I should, but I can if I want to – which means everything."

High:

"Having the confidence to do something I haven't done before. Being happy with my flaws, and knowing I've got some good stuff in my kit bag."

Low:

"After I exited GatenbySanderson, I was at a bit of a loss. I'd spent so much time thinking about the business and growing it that I didn't spend much time thinking about what came next. I'm too driven to feel comfortable with loads of downtime and no direction – I felt paralysed."

Golden nugget:

"What do you want from your business? What's important to you? Don't get so wrapped up in the running of your business that you lose sight of why you're doing it in the first place. Treat people fairly and consistently, and remember, no one knows everything. Once you understand that no one is better or worse than anyone else, it's much easier to manage people, sell products and services, and network your way forward."

Advice to others:

"Don't think, 'Why not?' Think, 'What if?' And don't believe everything people tell you – do your own research!"

26
BECOMING A SERIAL TECH ENTREPRENEUR AND ANGEL INVESTOR

Your network is your biggest asset to leverage

Sherry Coutu – Founders4Schools

By the time Sherry Coutu launched her business, Founders4Schools, she was already a seasoned entrepreneur and angel investor. This was to be her third business aimed at making life easier for a section of the population – this time, focused on young people.

Her previous companies were in the financial services industry (one was acquired, and the other floated on the Nasdaq and London Stock Exchange); Sherry had also been an initial investor in companies that are now household names – Lovefilm, Zoopla and LinkedIn.

The Founders4Schools enterprise, however, came from an issue she faced at home. She explains, "When my three children reached their teens, I became painfully aware of how ill-equipped they would be to navigate the world of work when the time came. Their schools had no time, training or tools to be able to instil the skills and information necessary – although working in education, they didn't seem to know about all the opportunities outside of the public sector."

Sherry created Founders4Schools as an ed-tech charity. The platform connects young people to successful business leaders in their community. Teachers have access, too, and can easily use it to create student–employer meetings. She explains, "More than 30,000 businesses have provided opportunities for 1,000,000+ students to date. It's easy to use. Students can even apply for and track work experiences on their phones using our Workfinder service." Using artificial intelligence and data science also means that the platform can make recommendations in a matter of seconds that would otherwise be invisible to the user – all at a fraction of the cost of doing it manually.

The driving force for Sherry was providing an understanding of how to help young people gain useful work-related skills: "There didn't seem to be anyone or anything helping or inspiring students to improve their employability, and they didn't know where they could turn to add to their skills. I know from experience how hard it is to recruit young people with the right attitude and skills, and I felt that the techniques and methods I'd used in previous businesses – which were all about connecting the right products and services to the people that needed them – could be applied to Founders4Schools."

There was a moment of hesitation though says Sherry, "I'd turned 50 at that point, and never thought I'd put my 'entrepreneurial hat' back on. But once I started talking to teachers, small business leaders and students about student prospects and the transition between education and work, I began to see that the platform wasn't just possible – it was necessary."

Customer recommendations have been plentiful, which doesn't surprise Sherry: "If your service works well, customers will be happy to tell their friends about it. The strength of the product, and the need for it, has always been the driver of further sales." Her research shows that 93% of bosses worry about taking on the right people – to such an extent that it keeps them up at night. That is an alarming statistic in itself, and contributes to the issue that most UK businesses are currently either static or shrinking. Yet that's one claim that doesn't match the rapid growth of Founders4Schools.

Funding the business wasn't a massive issue due to Sherry's sale of her previous investments and another subsequent sale. Being that it is a social enterprise, the tech industry was keen to support it on a pro-bono basis, which made a huge difference. Integration with LinkedIn and Duedil also made it possible to create tools for teachers and students to use to help them navigate their way to companies of all sizes that were hiring. The endorsement from the Department for Business, Energy and Industrial Strategy (BEIS) was a huge boost when it came. "The right elements were in place," says Sherry. "And once early users adopted the tool, we were able to implement their feedback to improve the product further. This helped us take it from a clunky first product to something people couldn't live without."

Sherry believes her team was instrumental during this stage. She explains, "I didn't want people around me who believed in perfection but it was important they had the same keen desire as me to delight users, to engage and improve, and to innovate." Fortunately, Sherry knew just the tool to find talent to hire due to her previous experience as an investor in LinkedIn, the world's largest professional networking platform. That's not to say it was easy, simply because as a charity, the company was trying to compete for engineering and data scientists against the likes of Facebook and Google.

Alongside these roles, Sherry continually builds her senior leadership team, which is another challenge. She says, "Though they're amazing, they've often worked for companies growing at a much slower speed. As a result, they can find some aspects of their role within Founders4Schools unfamiliar."

She upholds Professor Howard Stevenson's definition of an entrepreneur as a person who leverages resources they do not own or control to achieve something. *Forbes* magazine described Stevenson, the Sarofim-Rock Baker Foundation Professor Emeritus at Harvard University, as Harvard Business School's "lion of entrepreneurship" in a 2011 article.

"Having had successful businesses before, there wasn't much of a surprise. Entrepreneurship is exactly what I thought it would be – exhilarating and creative. If the problem is something worth solving – i.e. the skills gap – most people will want you to succeed."

Despite a fantastic portfolio of successful enterprises, Sherry doesn't believe she has the Midas touch. Not everything she touches turns to gold. In the past, she's backed ideas that didn't work out, although she says this quickly becomes apparent: "The trick is accepting when something hasn't worked, and to move on when you don't hear 'Yes, please' from customers."

Over the course of her entrepreneurial career, success has come to mean different things to Sherry. While it was exciting in her first business to make technologies used by institutional investors free to consumers – with a view to selling or floating the business further down the line – she sees Founders4Schools as something much more personal as her children are part of the faction she's helping. "Without the relevant attitude, skills and experience, a whole generation risks being left behind," she says. Sherry recalls her parents working in jobs they tolerated, and although this instilled a good work ethic within her, it didn't endear her to what lay ahead in the world of work once school was over.

"Maybe that's why I love being an entrepreneur. I find working with others to solve problems inspiring."

Sherry swims regularly and makes a point of walking between meetings as a way of clearing her mind and managing stress. Her commute between Cambridge and London gives her plenty of thinking time every day, which has provided her with the seeds of strategy she's so successfully ploughed into the business.

High:

"Nothing is better than hearing customers say they can't live without your product. The students at Stirling High School took it upon themselves to create a promotional video for us to use, because they felt we weren't shouting about it enough!"

Low:

"I find it difficult to say no, which can lead to being overwhelmed. Time is the true commodity in life, and I sometimes find myself without it."

Golden nugget:

"Richard E. Caruso, the founder and chairman of Integra Life Sciences and other companies, and renowned American entrepreneur, told me that in times of indecision, when you don't have enough information about the situation, it's still better to make a choice one way or the other and move forward than remaining static. I've lived by this for more than 30 years."

Advice to others:

"Your network is your biggest asset to leverage. The answers to problems don't lie in books –they lie within your peers and colleagues. I solve all my problems by talking them through with friends and the people in my network; it helps you find creative solutions."

GOLDEN RULES FOR EXITING YOUR BUSINESS

The women featured in this section of the book are the sages of entrepreneurs – they have fought the good fight and won. There are just a handful of women who have successfully exited their business and are now in the enviable position of being able to invest their time, energy and resources in others. We are fascinated by these women and their journeys. Their stories of determination, resilience and business acumen are featured in our local and national papers and magazines. They are the stars of TV programmes such as Shark Tank and the Dragons' Den. Their stories and example inspire us to pursue our version of entrepreneurial success regardless of our social status, age or profession.

Here is a summary of insights from this section:

1. Don't get greedy

Don't get greedy – owning 5% of a listed company is better than owning 100% of a shrinking business. Be open minded. There is always a way to make it work.

2. It is more than just work

Most women aspire to be women of leisure once they have exited their businesses. However, they find that they miss the hustle and bustle of running their businesses and the kinship they have built with their employees and colleagues. You will need a plan for life after you exit. It takes some adjustment to identify the right opportunities for your next chapter.

3. Keep moving forward

In times of indecision, when you don't have enough information about the situation, it's still better to make a choice one way or the other and move forward than remaining static. Just do something – no matter how uncertain you are – as it's far worse not to act.

4. Your network is your biggest asset

The answers to problems don't lie in books –they lie within your peers and colleagues. It is easier to arrive at a solution to challenging problems talking them through with friends and the people within your network. It is the easiest quickest way to find creative solutions to your problems.

5. Don't sell yourself short

If you're thinking about exiting your business, don't make any rash decisions, however tired you are or how much you think you want rid of it. Don't cut yourself off completely, because when it is gone, it is gone. Do not let yourself get burned out because this can lead to rash decision making.

6. Have an exit strategy

Start with the end in mind. Once you know what the end goal is, you will pick the right opportunities when they present themselves. An exit strategy enables you to maximise the opportunities and limit losses if things don't work out as planned.

7. Have a life plan

What is important to you outside of business? Most people feel at a loss once they exit their business. They spent so much time thinking about the business and growing it that they rarely think of life beyond the business. Spend time to reflect and think about what might come next for you. Most driven entrepreneurs do not feel comfortable with doing nothing. Don't get too wrapped up in the running of your business so that you lose sight of why you are doing it in the first place.

8. Don't dwell on it – move on

Not everything you touch after you exit your business will be successful. Some ideas and relationships will not work. Accepting when something is not working and moving on will save you a lot of stress and heartache. Some investments will be lost – but when investments do go well, it more than makes up for the losses.

9. Give back

It is important to give back whatever opportunities life has given us. We all learn so much on this journey of building your business that it should be an honour to help someone else achieve their own business dreams by sharing what we now know. This giving back mindset gives life purpose and meaning, which can be lost after exiting one's business.

10. Stay active

Even after exiting one's business, it is important to stay active to manage your health and wellbeing. No amount of wealth can buy you good health.

11. Never say never

It is never too late to step back into business as an entrepreneur especially when you spot a gap in the market, and you are inspired to be part of the solution. At this stage of your life, you now have the funds, the expertise and hopefully the time to make an even bigger success of it.

12. Always be humble

We all know women who have worked just as hard as we have, with the same dedication and commitment, who would have gone further but they have not had the same opportunities we had. Life is unfair and unjust in the way it unfolds. We all need to do the best with the cards we've been dealt whilst being mindful of others and their struggles.

THE UNSTOPPABLE MINDSET

Masks on first

An unstoppable mindset makes you unstoppable. It gives you freedom, focus, energy, headspace, and the physical and mental resilience to keep going after your goals even when others quit. Unstoppable women understand that they need to put their own gas mask on first before they can support others. Developing the unstoppable mindset is your key to achieving your goals. Unstoppable women are special because they embody the unstoppable mindset.

Mindset 1: Everyone sees a challenge or barrier as a stop sign; unstoppable women see barriers as hurdles they can jump over or crawl under. Won't the banks lend to you? No problem. Explore other options such as crowdfunding because no one will get in your way to achieve your goals.

Mindset 2: Everyone else sees problems, but unstoppable women see opportunities. They don't leave societal issues for someone else to solve. They double down and figure out a way to change the world and create a positive impact. Do you spot a gap in the market for a product you desperately need to make your life easier? Unstoppable women will go ahead and create the solutions they are looking for.

Mindset 3: Whilst everyone else is looking for short-term gratification, unstoppable women know to defer gratification until the work is completed. Unstoppable women understand that the rewards are sweetest after the work is completed.

Mindset 4: Everyone else is waiting to feel 100% confident about an opportunity before making their move. Unstoppable women make their move because they understand that feeling total confidence 100% of the time is a myth. Confidence is a muscle that needs exercising.

Mindset 5: Unstoppable women make the best decision with the information they have and know they can course-correct as new information becomes available. Whilst everyone else allows others to manage their finances, money and investments, unstoppable women remain in control of their finances. They are not afraid to ask tough, uncomfortable questions and to take steps to protect their assets. They strive for financial literacy and feel comfortable reading their balance sheet and profit and loss statements. They take pride in their financial literacy and surround themselves with trusted advisors. They invest in their financial future.

Mindset 6: Unstoppable women prioritize themselves and their dreams because they believe they are worthy and have something to contribute and value to add to the world. They don't need to burn themselves out trying to be the perfect friend, wife, boss etc. They understand that the people who matter and whose opinions count will understand when they have to take a rain check and reorganize priorities. They are not constantly chasing external public validation. Unstoppable women prioritize their mental health and well-being. They get the help they need, whether it is therapy or counselling. They read books, join support groups and networks and recognize the fragility of our minds. They take breaks and vacations and disconnect from work to give their mind the break it needs. Being always switched on because you feel your business cannot run without you is not healthy. Your health is your greatest asset. Unstoppable women protect their health.

Mindset 7: Unstoppable women are protective of their time and energy and have healthy boundaries around them. They make time to think because being a business owner requires an alert mind and clarity of thought. Unstoppable women understand that social media is a tool. Whilst everyone else is happy to be distracted by social media notifications and unscheduled mindless chitchat, unstoppable women manage their time and use technology to get more done in less time. They create distraction-free zones that enable them to produce their best work. They do not allow technology to determine their schedules or distract them from their goals.

Mindset 8: Unstoppable women are not trying to do all things themselves. They know they are not superhuman. Once they can afford to, they delegate areas of their lives that can be delegated. You don't need to be the cook, the perfect volunteer, cleaner, etc. Share the responsibility with your significant others. Nannies, PAs, cleaners, bookkeepers and all kinds of virtual support are available to help make your life easier. Use them by finding one that fits your budget.

Mindset 9: Unstoppable women have a CEO mindset. They are committed to working on their businesses and on themselves. They are not afraid to invest in their personal development. They also do not use training courses and personal development to procrastinate and avoid doing the work that needs to be done. Unstoppable women understand that business is a team sport. They invest in building up by relationships, networks and support systems that can help them achieve their goals. They have strong social and professional networks who they feel connected to – like we have here at forwardladies.com.

Mindset 10: Unstoppable women understand that bias and sexism is rife in our patriarchal society, but they do not allow it to stop them. Unstoppable women do not internalize society's limited belief about the role of women and men. They understand that their particular situation is unique and might need a different approach to make things work for them.

Mindset 11: Unstoppable women understand that perfection is a myth. In our society, young girls are frequently fed stories that linger into adulthood. From a young age, girls are socialised to be perfect and not to be brave, to be quiet and not to speak up, to be seen but not heard. This phenomenon sadly prevails across all cultures. Unfortunately, such socialised ideas often remain buried in our psyches until we do the personal development work needed to push us past these unconscious but powerful barriers.

Adopting the unstoppable women mindset is simple but takes courage. It is also entirely up to you. You can keep following the crowd – the 97% who are unsatisfied with their lives – or you can decide to unleash your unstoppable self. You have a choice. Every day, you get to exercise that choice. So, if you want more and are currently not satisfied with your life right now, you have the option to choose to be unstoppable.

Start today, start now. The choice is yours.

AFTERWORD: WHAT'S NEXT?

Make the rest of your life the best of your life

We women are all so unique and special – our stories are rich and beautifully diverse. There is not one single path to success, as you have seen from the stories of our unstoppable women. We all have choices and opportunities presented to us at different phases of our lives, and we just need to make the best with what we have. Failure can be the building blocks of success. We can all identify with the fear of failure – even sometimes, the fear of success – and the pressures we face as we try to define what success ultimately means to us. This is a daily struggle, so it is reassuring to see that despite the challenges, some women have not only made it, but are still making it. They are pushing on and remaining *unstoppable*. Seeing how they did it is important as it can help give you the confidence and inspiration to chase your own dreams – but you will need to find your own way to do it and on your own terms if you want to enjoy the journey and to create a path to success that is meaningful to you.

Our success hinges on people – those who mentor us, those who help us build our businesses and those who support us when the going gets tough. Being an entrepreneur can be a lonely existence. Few people understand what you are going through unless they have done it themselves, so do surround yourself with a network of other entrepreneurs who can understand your struggles and help you get through the tough days.

Together, we *can* be unstoppable. Let's be unstoppable together at forwardladies.com.

Griselda Togobo

YOUR UNSTOPPABLE JOURNAL: WHAT'S NEXT FOR YOU?

This section is an invitation to you – it's a place for you to reflect, plan and visualise your unstoppable self.

I've included questions and prompts just as we did with the women featured in this book, which I hope will help spark the process of introspection and reflection that will help you on your unstoppable journey. There are no right or wrong answers – it is just your life, in all its glorious beauty and messiness.

What does being "unstoppable" mean to you?

What are your highs?

What are your lows?

What golden nuggets have you learned from your experiences?

What advice would you give to others?

What aspects of this book did you like the most, and why?

What is the one thing you plan to do after reading this book that will help you to achieve your goals?

How are you going to build a strong, supportive network around you?

ACKNOWLEDGEMENTS

Thanks to the wonderful members and team at forwardladies.com

FREE RESOURCES & BONUSES

Connect with mission-driven women
and download your FREE resources with your 14-day
trial at: www.forwardladies.com/join-us/

If you like this book,

please give it a 5-star review on Amazon.

With *Unstoppable Women*, Griselda Togobo has set out to inspire and motivate female entrepreneurs of the future by sharing the stories of the many successful female businesswomen of today to show how you, too, can gain the strength, wisdom, determination and resilience you need to succeed in what is still largely a man's world.

Each of the women profiled openly and candidly shares their journeys – from having the initial concept for their business to the early stages of developing, growing and seeing their profits escalate, to the further stages of scaling-up and even exiting their businesses, with some ultimately moving on to 'give back' by becoming angel investors and mentors to others. Their stories provide invaluable 'golden nuggets' and advice to other women to help them with each phase of starting out, developing and moving on after realising their entrepreneurial dreams.

Along with the inspiring stories of these successful entrepreneurs, there are overview sections that effectively distil the learnings from each phase, and a workbook section for you to use to record and plan your own journey so that you, too, will become unstoppable. The book is an excellent tool to enable women from all walks of life fulfil their dreams and manage their journey to success.

Printed in Great Britain
by Amazon

28033321R00138